W9-BRA-879

Imagining Families:
Images and Voices

The National African American Museum   A Smithsonian Institution Project

Contents

© 1994 by the Smithsonian Institution. All rights reserved. No part of this book may be reproduced in any form or by any means, electronic or mechanical, including photocopying, recording, or by any information storage and retrieval system, without permission in writing from the Publisher.

Published by the National African American Museum, A Smithsonian Institution Project, Smithsonian Institution, Washington DC.

Author: Deborah Willis
Text Editor: Jane Lusaka
Design: John Morning

Library of Congress Cataloging-in-Publication Data

ISBN 1-885892-00-4
1. Exhibition catalogs.   2. Photography.   3. Art.
I. Willis, Deborah.
II. Title: Imagining Families: Images and Voices.

Library of Congress Catalog Card Number: 94-67719

Foreword

The National African American Museum at the Smithsonian Institution will function as a three-dimensional family album for a large and extended family. It will contain our ancestors and our contemporaries in their struggle to attain dignity and personal success. We will save and preserve objects made by our own hands, the tools of our labor and the artistic gifts that we have given to society at large.

The National African American Museum's inaugural exhibition, *Imagining Families: Images and Voices* was curated, in part, as a response to the many Americans who have contacted the Smithsonian Institution to express their interest in making a meaningful contribution to the planned National African American Museum.

In the Spring of 1991, the Regents of the Smithsonian Institution gave their conditional endorsement for the proposed National African American Museum. Their support was conditional because they were not sure that there were sufficient private collections that might be donated to the museum. Some assumed that African American material culture was already safely ensconced in American museum collections throughout the nation. There was also the firmly held belief within the museum profession that working class people use their objects until they use them up. In the case of the African American community, neither theory proved to be true.

Between 1991 and 1992, I identified approximately 300 collectors who had accumulated more than 20,000 artifacts and documents related to the history and culture of persons of African descent in the United States and throughout the African diaspora.

In 1992 Deborah Willis joined the National African American Museum Project staff as Collections Coordinator. She has continued to identify and document pivotal collections here and abroad. During the course of our identification effort, both Deborah and I have encountered collectors whose photograph albums give context and meaning to the stories they tell and provide the viewer with a better understanding of the role of an object in a historical moment.

We have also encountered photo-journalists and hobbyists who have documented our contemporary history; and artists who have captured the passion and emotion of pivotal political, social and cultural movements in their photographic works. As is often the case in this profession, we saw more work than we will ever be able to collect. However, the events which these photographs and artifacts elucidate are significant to those persons who were affected by them; and many of these objects may find a home in local or regional institutions.

Early in our work we recognized the importance of family members as primary preservers of cultural patrimony. Family collections are sometimes passed down through several generations before they make their home in a museum.

Accordingly, we have made a commitment to acquaint families with collections care practices and to encourage them to document their family histories. We have used our newsletter, *Orator,* as a vehicle for helping our constituency to actively accept responsibility for preserving African American material culture in their homes, businesses, places of worship, and communities.

Imagining Families: Images and Voices allows us to glimpse lifestories. We are invited into the hearts and homes of 15 artists whose photographs demand that we consider familial relationships and the roles that individuals play in communities. This visual testimonial exhibition allows each viewer to step inside a community that may be different, from one's own, and confront a world that can pose the same challenges for each of us. *Imagining Families: Images and Voices* enables us to witness the many different perceptions of family and encourages us to listen to the myriad voices that claim us as kin.

—Claudine Brown
Deputy Assistant Secretary
for the Arts and Humanities,
Smithsonian Institution

Visual Memories

Consider this passage from Peter Galassi's *Pleasures and Terrors of Domestic Comfort:*

Perhaps the most ubiquitous of all photographs, snapshots are also the most hermetic. To the insider, to the member of the family, snapshots are keys that open reservoirs of memory and feeling. To the outsider, who does not recognize the faces or know the stories, they are forever opaque. At the same time, because we all have snapshots of our own, and thus know the habit of understanding them, we all are equipped to imagine ourselves into the snapshots of others, into the dreams and the passions they conceal.[1]

These words, I believe, easily express the thoughts and works produced by the photoartists in *Imagining Families: Images and Voices.* As I research and write about photographic images that relate to family stories, I often encounter poets, writers, painters and photographers who use the family theme as a position from which to create text, images and installation art. Over the past four years I have witnessed an overwhelming number of photography curators, like Galassi, who have organized in their own museums and galleries, powerful and engaging exhibitions relating to "the family." Exhibitions such as *Home and Other Stories, The Visual Diary, Disputed Identities, U.K./U.S., The Family As Subject, Disclosing the Myth of Family*, and *Memories of Home*, have been hosted and displayed around the country and have placed the

family at the center of creating art and further anchored the social role of photography in art practices. We can no longer look at family and archival photographs without considering them in a historical context—whether it be personal or social. Studying photographs as a point of departure has inspired me to place the works and words of diverse photographic artists in a forum where a museum-going public would be able to consider their own family photographs in a more innovative context.

Imagining Families: Images And Voices is that exhibition. Fifteen photographic artists speak from diverse cultural perspectives about race, class and gender. All are linked by the improvisational telling of a story through the photographic medium. We are asked to discover and uncover. We are invited to ponder, imagine, and explore love, loss, rejection, greed and controversy. The ideas realized in this exhibition by the artists can also be linked to the writings of family therapist Alan D. Entin, who uses family photographs to discover "who, what, where, when, and how the family chooses to document its existence as a family." Many of his articles discuss the relationship of family photographs to psychotherapy. "Photographs contain a wealth of information," he writes. "Not only are the images and relationships depicted important; so too, are the spaces around the pictures. The background can be read as information about social-cultural values, traditions, and ideals. Photographs tell not only about what is photographed but about who is doing the photographing. Photographs are biographical as well as autobiographical."[2]

This is the first exhibition organized by the National African American Museum Project. *Imagining Families: Images and Voices* was inspired by one of our mission goals—which is to interpret family history within the larger American historical research confines. *Imagining Families: Images and Voices* contains selected family and archival photographs, installation art and slide projected images from 15 contemporary American photographers who are making larger statements about American family life during the 19th and 20th centuries. It reveals personal, private moments as well as re-stages events, both lived and imagined. Many of the photographs were taken by the exhibiting artists; some were taken by family members or friends. At the heart of many of the works are encoded messages in which the photoartists document their own perceptions and remembrances of their personal and family lives as well as the larger lives of their various communities. The result is a private testimonial with broader, more public implications for a generation coming to terms with the latent spiritual influences of family life. Whether complex or supportive, disparate or similar, familial experiences throughout this country all share the retentive nature of both the old and new worlds, of family values, and of survival.

Imagining Families: Images and Voices brings together works by photographic artists Albert Chong, Fay Fairbrother, Lonnie Graham, David Keating, Lynn Marshall-Linnemeier, Fern Logan, Lorie Novak, Lorna Simpson, Clarissa Sligh, Margaret Stratton, Diane Tani, Christian Walker, Carrie Mae Weems, Pat Ward Williams, and Florence Flo Oy Wong. Most of them use snapshots to create symbolic references within their art. All are engaging storytellers and have discovered the intersection of the private and public in art; they direct our gaze through a seemingly-tinted veil. Their art has evolved beyond the personal, pedestrian text/image narrative to a more powerful, universal and reflective realm of discourse. They change our notions of displacement, isolation and disenfranchisement. These photoartists were selected because their art has challenged contemporary art practices and they have created, in the words of photographer/writer Rick Bolton, "a new social basis for art."[3]

This exhibition is an important first for the National African American Museum Project because it describes the way in which we hope to engage the American public about its past, its burgeoning aspiration, and how it defines its present self. We see this exhibition as an inclusive one that authenticates personal experiences within the larger American cultural experience.

Imagining Families: Images and Voices will focus on pictures that are made, created and re-interpreted. The 15 artists are photobiographers who use appropriation, multiple printing, fabric, straight images, interactive slide projection, and manipulated photographs to make compelling visual statements about modern day culture as well as create narratives about our collective history in this multi-ethnic society. These photobiographers employ themes relating to gender, family, race, differences, and stereotypes. Some are concerned with the implications of historical and contemporary references to women and incorporate personal perspectives and offer new strategies in the construction of their work. They stage fictive narratives, restage events, use text, and create traditional photographs to shape psychological tensions as well as paradigms related to the transformation of the family.

These are diverse points of view of provocative photoartists working today, who are creating a different photographic expression that cannot be ignored or overlooked. Their work offers a strikingly different perspective from that of many photographic exhibitions largely because these artists are physically involved in the telling of these often humorous stories and are unmasking repressive behavior in order to enlighten us about family realities. Their family structures are different, yet the stories they create are similar and are constructed with descriptive captions, recognizable to us all. Issues referring to gender and identity are key concerns. Like a biography, *Imagining Families: Images and Voices* aims to explore the various voices and the collective ide-

ological concerns of the narrators/artists. We hope that this exhibition will be viewed and read in the context of a forum which will encourage provocative discussion about photography and family.

Albert Chong
uses family photographs, religious icons, and animal remains to explore ritual as it is translated into art. He is like an archaeologist, unearthing the past to explore family history. Chong is strongly conscious of composition and form. His exact placement of cultural objects acts as a signifier of his cultural roots and suggests authenticity. Born in Jamaica of African and Chinese ancestry, Chong's works are imbued with cultural references relating to both, as well as references to the Caribbean. He is obviously aware of the differences, but he draws our attention to the similar ritual practices. Writer and poet, Quincy Troupe aptly points out the cultural basis behind Chong's work: "There is magic, music, myth and mystery in photographs of Albert Chong because he sees and creates it within his frames: after all, the whole point of photography is seeing and Albert Chong sees very well. But Chong also interprets and feels what is before him in a magical and musical way. The way he composes within his photographic frame is similar to a musical composition—many of his prints are a little off center in the same way that much of

great music is played off the beat. Like searching on the piano for the flatted 5th, music is created by Chong's constant interplay with dark and light. Sometimes dissonant, sometimes luminous, sometimes rough around the edges, his creations are always challenging for the eye."[4] Speaking about *The Sisters,* Chong states:

Several years ago, my mother sent me the only remaining picture of herself as child—an old torn and yellowing photograph of three girls. She is the smallest child in the picture; the other two girls are her cousins. She asked me to repair the picture. I could not heal it, but I could re-photograph it incorporating the torn area of the image.

While re-photographing the picture, I became overwhelmed by the simple beauty of the image in its recording of three sisters of African-Chinese ancestry as they poised themselves for history. Jamaica was a mere sixty years out of slavery, and she was an orphan at the time. Her father, a Chinese musician, had died in his sleep while she played in the bed around his body. Her mother had left Jamaica when she was an infant to live with a man in Honduras. She learned of her mother's death months after the fact—that she had died of hemorrhaging caused by fright, as her man tried to play a joke on her.

I thought of the importance of this photograph to her, how as a child it must have been an affirmation of her existence, if only to her. I thought of the many old historical photographs I had seen, and of the fact that few contained people of color. I realized in that instant how inconsequential this photograph, and the lives that it illuminates, was to white civilization. I knew that I could not merely copy this picture, that it meant too

much and should remain in the world meaning something to others. In this spirit of cultural retrieval, "The Sisters" emerged.

The photographs of Albert Chong are highly individualized, spiritually oriented images. The piece titled *Throne for Mr. Baker,* in homage to Chong's father, illustrates the depth of their familial relationship. The series *The Thrones for the Ancestors* further exemplifies Chong's incorporation of personal objects in the production of individualized images that affirm his relationship to his ancestors. Curator Thelma Golden responds to Chong's throne series thusly: "While his father's physical presence marks some of these works through Chong's centralized use of his image, other thrones conjure specific spirits. The constituent ideas which inform *The Thrones for the Ancestors* are intertwined with Chong's consistent reckoning with death and desire for communion with his ancestors. While the *Justice* subtext embraces a literal homage to his father, a more metaphoric exploration of his ancestry moves throughout Chong's various genres."[5]

Fay Fairbrother also addresses
issues concerning family strengths, fears, failures, and successes in her art. She openly explores repression and racism through the art of quilt-making. Fairbrother's *The Shroud Series: Quilt Shroud, I and II* include turn-of-the-

century formal portraits of black and white families, images of black men who were lynched and mutilated, and shots of Ku Klux Klan activities—all on patterned cloth. One quilt juxtaposes family images with photographs of KKK activities, which document the participation of the wives and children of Klan members. The pictures reproduced in the quilt create a patchwork of events depicting the injustices and privileges of two distinct families—black and white.

The Quilt Shroud series was titled after Fairbrother, who lives in Stillwater, Oklahoma, did comprehensive research on lynchings of African American men. Fairbrother's extensive research revealed that, following their gruesome deaths, lynched men were wrapped in quilts in preparation for burial by their families. Her use of quilts is powerful and disarming. Using cloth fragments to tell a story of an anonymous family, Fairbrother creates an arena for contemplation. There are questions suggested and left unanswered regarding segregation, life and death, family structure and photography's role in depicting ordinary domestic life and racial violence in America. As Fairbrother describes,

The theme of *The Quilt Shroud I* is the family, with the quilt as a representation of family. The posed studio portraits of black and white families illustrate the sameness of the family group. Posed in their Sunday best, you know the children are taught the same Christian values and morals. But where does the process go wrong with Ku Klux Klan meetings, such as the one illustrated on the third row, resulting in black men hanging from trees? I have also tried to show the results of the removal of the black man from his family and the wife shown alone in the studio with their child who has been robbed of his father. The quilts are my own design, kept simple in order for the photographs to speak.

Like many of our mothers and grandmothers before us, Fairbrother's ancestors were quilt-makers. She is a third-generation quilter; the tradition was handed down to her by her mother. Fairbrother grew up in a white middle class environment in the South. Harsh stories about racial violence within her own community were told to her by members of her family. In re-examining these stories about the African American community, Fairbrother expands the notion of self-portrait by creating a wider portrait of her community and documents how memory helped to shape her art in a social context.

Lonnie Graham

is a photographer who has cogently expanded the domain of portraiture from a mere reflection to a fully-realized portrait of an individual. In creating *Aunt Dora's Room* from the installation *Living In A Spirit House,* Graham assumes the role of biographer. The viewer is invited into a space that is spiritually connected to the artist. Kimberly Camp states:

Lonnie Graham believes that his life and his work are about making an investment in the spiritual past. That investment manifests in his on-going dialogue with his ancestors, as he weaves a tale of love, integrity, honesty, and mystery using the camera and film as parts of the tapestry. Graham sensitively, yet assertively, examines the context of the creative process with the tangible elements that comprise the very character of a place.[6]

Refining the genre of his own portrait photography, Graham produces an introspective quality in his vision. His installation is a collaboration with the spiritual past and the familiar. He creates a solitude for reflection. The image of Aunt Dora framed in the doorway reminds us of the continuum. Committed to ensuring that the spiritual connection is still a part of his work process, Graham includes household items that reveal Aunt Dora's aesthetic appreciation. His use of crocheted doilies, floral arrangements, and framed family portraits is an attempt to introduce us to the spiritual comfort that embraces the room.

When asked what motivated him to create this piece, Graham stated:

By committing myself to this work, I feel I have managed to address issues of relevance to a broader audience, by establishing a visual and tangible narrative that is not afield of the psychological, spiritual, and physical experience of the viewing audience. In this way, the work becomes completely relevant. All of the viewer's senses are stimulated: sight, mind, touch, smell, and auditory scenes.

Aunt Dora's Room is a remarkable way for a photographer to recall his past and to contemplate about how his art is produced.

David Keating's photographs are

self-consciously composed and carefully constructed. He began photographing to make a record of the world around him. "I thought of photography not as a means of self-expression but as a way to document," he says.

However, I did sense that photographs had a life of their own. I was fascinated by certain family photographs, often without knowing who took them, when, or why. After years of making my own photographs, I began to think about family photographs again. If these images had as much meaning for me as my own, why not use them in my work? In fact, I realized, I could make use of all manner of found imagery, memorabilia, and text. Much of my current work is rooted in family politics, As I grew up, there was an enormous amount of denial in my family. Emphasis was placed on propriety at the expense of honesty and emotional well-being. I was taught to live my life in other people's minds. What would the neighbors think? In our community this attitude translated into rampant snobbery and prejudice. Playing along was hateful and self-destructive. I am tired of that denial. By labeling it and exposing it, I can come to terms with myself.

Keating's work involves photography, text, and installation. His images address both specific and autobiographical concerns and push private issues to the surface. The transient, domestic images in *Troth* explore this idea. As Keating states:

Troth is the piece about my parents' divorce . . . It hangs on the wall so that the diagonal recession in the photos suggests a giant "X". The text is engraved in formal wedding invitation type on magnesium panels. There is a poem written by my mother inset over the central picture . . . The poem reads:

ODE TO P.K.
He's six feet tall and his chest is hairy,
And he knows all the words in the dictionary.
His face is noble and his brow serene,
He's the handsomest fellow I've ever seen.
A month ago I took his hand,
Danced from the ranks of the spinster band.
And don't you think I've ever regretted,
The fact that we wuz finally wedded.
The truth of the matter, as plain to see,
Is that I'm as happy as a bumble bee
(Cause I love my honey
And my honey loves me.)

For me, the idea behind the piece was how money and objects got in the way of a proper expression of love in our family. The gifts display the shiny promise of a new marriage, and the text reveals its dissolution. This is the most expensive piece I have made, which seemed only fitting.

Keating invests his photographs with domestic and pro-fessional descriptive language. In *Family Legend,* the family patriarch is both a privileged idealized figure and a complicated man with multiple identities. According to Keating,

Family Legend is based on my great-grandfather. My father's family held him up as a paragon, but my mother and a cousin who did biographical research on him had quite another view. The photograph is enlarged from a postcard he made of himself in a studio on the Atlantic City boardwalk. Below it I made a list of the positions and titles that he held in his lifetime. (Actually, he held even more positions, but it became ridiculous to list them all, and they probably required that he show up once a year to vote a board meeting.) The list becomes increasingly less flattering as it is punctuated with his other roles (chauvinist, anticommunist, anti-Semite, bigot, sexist, homophobe).

The collective family memory is witnessed within the Keating's family critique.

The images made by Chicago-based

Fern Logan

are a photographic construction of her relationship with her son and daughter. Logan re-examines the relationships through her art. Using the cyanotype (also known as the blueprint process, a printing process based on the light sensitivity of iron salts),

Logan critiques memories from her past in a warm voice using old letters and imagined responses. Looking back at old photographs of her son, she draws up provocative issues about his American childhood and the irony of his fate. Her emotions are written on the print as the image becomes submerged. The issues presented are difficult and evoke a 20th century consciousness of miscegenation. Forced to come to consciousness because of the issues presented within her own family, Logan stimulates an open discussion about race, racism, denial and domination. *American Hero* incorporates two letters and a photograph; the handwritten text on the cyanotype reads:

My son is ashamed of me. He acts out his shame in anger. He doesn't call me on my birthday; he doesn't send me a card on Mother's day; I don't hear from him on Christmas, Easter, Valentine's Day, or any other day. He is ashamed of me because I am Black. He has never openly accused me of giving him his shaded tint and curly hair; blame and silence are his weapons of choice. I remember the times before the shame, before he spent his teenage years with his white father in a small middle American town. I remember when he used to tell me he loved me. I blame myself for not revealing the truth to him at an early age. It was my responsibility to relate pride in the African American heritage. But I was raised to believe in "liberty and justice for all." I truly had no idea how rampant the racist ethic really was in this country. It was interesting that people said, "What about the children?" when I married his father. I didn't know what they were talking about.

American Hero provides a visual fragmentation of a covert set of circumstances undermining the relationship of a mother and her son. More important, it creates a forum for families to openly create a venue for exchange. *Questions* also incorporates social and personal commentary on the effects of racism on her family. Its narrative explores the heated accusations a conflicted man of mixed race faces when he chooses to date a white woman. Both works share Logan's painful reactions to the effects of racism on her children "who have in many ways have internalized the racist ethic of our day."

The series by **Lynn Marshall-Linnemeier** titled *Sanctuary* (1991) is a fictionalized historical narrative centered around the community of Mound Bayou, Mississippi. Mound Bayou, one of the oldest African American communities in the United States, was founded by former slaves. Marshall-Linnemeier began the *Sanctuary* series in 1990 while working on a collaborative documentary project in Mound Bayou for the Center for Southern Folklore in Jackson, Mississippi and the Center for Documentary Studies at Duke University in Durham, North Carolina. She found old photographs taken by a former Mound Bayou resident, Mattie "Goldie" Thompson. During her lifetime, Goldie took hundreds of photographs and captioned them with descriptive prose.

Marshall-Linnemeier was inspired by the photographs and began to combine the stories with contemporary images she produced while photographing in Mound Bayou. *Sanctuary* reflects the soothing comfort that family stories and mythology can provide. One of her first photographs, *The Genie,* is of a young man who posed for her. With his arms crossed and an inquisitive smile, he reminded her of a genie. She then created a story in which this street genie could use his magic. According to Marshall-Linnemeier:

In 1990, my father died. I turned to Mound Bayou and its people, as well as my own family, for comfort. I was welcomed with open arms. Feeling the need to express creatively, my feelings about the kindness shown to me and the importance of Mound Bayou in my life, *Sanctuary* was born—my first series combining photography, paint and narrative.

In *Sometimes I Hear Voices,* Marshall-Linnemeier places photographic images in different planes and creates multiple imagery. As she overlays suggestive mythological references, Marshall-Linnemeier enables the viewer to imagine the experiences staged within the frame. The addition of hand painting and multiple printing creates an allegorical portrayal of an artist as one who refuses to break ties with the past. *Sometimes I Hear Voices* represents the bonding Marshall-Linnemeier realized with families while looking at their photo albums. Says the artist:

The people and places contained in those albums were like archetypes of my own family and my hometown, Southern Pines, North Carolina, supporting my belief that our ancestors, through some mystical, psychical, and perhaps even genetic connection, call out to us in times of trouble and joy.

Since the early 1980s,

Lorie Novak

has been working with projected imagery. Like many of the other photographic artists in this exhibition, she uses her own family album as well as albums of others in her work. In using images from photographic albums—both formal and candid portraits—Novak responds consciously to each individual image. She is not only looking at the subject photographed; she also projects the thoughts of the person holding the camera. Through the use of projected images, Lorie Novak simulates poetry in motion. Novak's work reminds us of a visual memory—a collected memory that we all share—of moments in our lives. Diana du Pont writes, "By extension, physical projection leads to psychological projection wherein the viewer can begin to see in Novak's imagery aspects of his/her own past."[7] Novak herself has stated, "I am interested in the relationships between photographic images, particularly how personal and collective memory affect our visual perception and reading of photographs."[8]

In an interview with Rene Paul Barilleaux, Novak reflects on her work process:

As soon as I began physically projecting slides indoors, I became aware that I was "projecting" emotions and thoughts into the rooms. My early interests were directly related to this idea—when you walk into a room, when you go to any new place, you bring with you all sorts of visual images that you have in your memory. I could make this idea of memory materialize. The relationship between memory and photographs has always interested me—photographs as substitutes for memory and as "evidence" of a past. I think the emotional impact of my photographs is dependent on the fact that photographs do trigger associations with the past. . . . Because the family images have personal meaning to me, I understand them and have perspective on them. I want the final photographs to comment on families and their myths, so I think the repetition of the same people is important. I feel that by projecting slides into any situation, I am raising questions as to what is real.[9]

Novak again combines family images and music in her slide installation called *Collected Visions,* commissioned in 1993 by the Houston Center for Photography. This piece examines the representation of women and girls in family photographs and the experience of growing up female. The artist incorporates the images of over 75 women from varied backgrounds and different generations. Parts I and II are ten minute sequences representing girlhood and the experience of coming of age. The third sequence chronologically traces the maturation

from girl to adolescence. Subtleties of gaze and gesture become clues for how girls begin to find their personal voice and the layering of images within and between sequences emphasizes the complexities of representation. In Sequence I, a woman's hands, holding open books about women (such as *A Room of One's Own, Little Women, Talking Back,* and *Writing a Woman's Life*), are superimposed over many of the images. Simultaneously, the third sequence unfolds in an opposite corner with images dissolving from wall to wall. The joys and angst of growing up become recollected through this blend of images and music.

Lorie Novak's projected images reconstruct the family snapshot into an image interwoven with the complexities of each pictured individual, the individual's relation to the family unit, and the family's capacity and connection to society. Composer Elizabeth Brown created a score for the installation. Brown describes their collaborative process:

I watched Lorie's sequences at various points to get a feel for the mood—*poignant* seems close. I thought about the aural equivalent of the dissolve, which in its simplest form is overlapping resonance. The music accomplishes this in several ways: the instruments themselves are very resonant (the viola d'amore has seven "sympathetic" strings, which make an aura above its sound, for example); the music is written with overlapping time values; and it was recorded in a very resonate space (The Church of the Good Shepherd in Manhattan).

Lorna Simpson

focuses on the construction of meaning and values by juxtaposing text and image. Her style creates a format for her critical examination of race and gender. She focuses specifically on the notion of invisibility, representing black women as survivors, protagonists and victims. Simpson's work is rooted in the tradition of African American storytelling. Her work incorporates visual narratives that border on biography. Simpson's photographs are sculptural, dramatic and anchored to a collective memory of events that is cross-generational. She has pushed the perimeters of autobiography in photography beyond their previous limits, and she has forcefully presented complex issues in a style radically divorced from the documentary conventions with which photography is most associated.[10] Says the artist:

It occurred to me that the modern fascination with African masks involved the front of a mask and its formal, geometric qualities. But the idea of contemplating the mask from *behind* brings the viewer closer to the cultural involvement that the mask represents. It speaks of a participatory ritual or performance. But who is the performer and what is being performed? This idea got me interested in dealing with the backs of the masks.[11]

Coiffure (1991), three black and white large scale photographs hung as a triptych, is a self-conscious piece. The images include the back of a woman's closely cropped hair, a segment of a long braid wrapped in a spiral and the back of an African mask. They are displayed with ten engraved plaques with short phrases referring to hair. Simpson explores the evocative potential of black representations in hair by placing the images and text in manner that invites the viewer to experience the references in the narrative. Coco Fusco has critiqued Simpson's use and placement of masks: "[. . . P]resentation of the back of the mask is carried over into many of Simpson's latest works, wherein African masks are continuously reversed to show their insides. While the artist stressed in our interview that she chose to reverse the masks to recodify their meaning by unseating their conventional reception as a beautiful object, I would argue that this inversion also invites the spectator to see him/herself as its potential wearer. Placing this relationship at the heart of the experience of viewing, Simpson calls upon us to reflect on our relationship to this icon of African-ness at a critical juncture in black American thought when the pros and cons of Afrocentrism are debated daily."[12]

Clarissa Sligh's

work is layered with suggestive messages. She incorporates politics into her art. Using family photographs and archival references, she directs her audience to gaze into sociological relationships based on experiences in African American communities in the 19th and 20th centuries. Sligh is the keeper of her family's photograph albums and other memorabilia. She is cognizant of the role she plays in preserving her family history. She places her family's story within the larger picture of American history. In shifting attention away from her personal experiences, she analyzes shared experiences of black children across generations.

In *Reading Dick and Jane With Me,* Sligh reconstructs the images of Dick and Jane with snapshots from her family album. The standard American public school Dick-and-Jane-type readers, which were published from 1935 to 1965, presented the typical American family as well-to-do WASPS living a trouble-free life. *Reading Dick and Jane With Me* is an illustrated reader seen through the eyes of a black woman artist who spent her own childhood growing up poor in the American south of the 1940s and 1950s. It combines lively repetitive words, photographs, and drawings. Sligh "reads" the images of Dick and Jane and inserts new words on each page, for example: "You play in your good clothes every page. We must keep ours nice for Sunday School days." She focuses our attention on the psychological effect that the primary school reader may have had on other black children reading the book. She allows the invisible black child to be identifiable as well as visible. In the words of the artist:

As a young black child, before I could even think, I was told how bad things are out there in the world for us. It was a

fear put into me to prepare me for the real world. Since we couldn't talk about it, since no one could relate to our hurt or pain, we learned to be silent, to hide our disappointments, to hide our anger at the distortion of our identity and the exclusion of our reality.

Sligh's work is important not only because she addresses the realities of racism and sexism in a direct yet not confrontational style, but also because she is an accomplished storyteller. The search for representation continues throughout her work. As Sligh explains,

My work is a journey toward self-change which itself is self-healing. The act of creating my visual statements requires that I work from a place I push against. I begin by trying to be clear with myself. I struggle to develop a correct relationship to myself, a continuous cycle requiring passage through darkness—my 'shadow areas'—as well as through light.

Sligh looks carefully at her own relationships with her family as she re-examines the lives of men, women and children in general.

Sligh's images reflect both historical and social perspectives. Her work is provocative and historically introspective. Themes pertaining to free blacks and enslaved Africans are part of her current work. "*Sandy Ground* is the exploration which questions relationships, identity, beliefs, and my own authenticity," Sligh says. "It also takes shape from my dreams, my subconscious, and my perceptions of past and present experiences." In 1820, a free black woman, Eliza Morriss (age 20) purchased a slave, Philip Cooler (age 26), from his owners. They married and had five children. Through hard work, the Coolers (who later changed their name to Cooley) accumulated a fair amount of real and personal property. Sandy Ground is the historic fishing village in Staten Island, New York, where the Coolers lived; one of the oldest surviving settlements of freed African Americans in the nation. It was a community strengthened by its church and its history, marked by relative prosperity and by misfortune.

Sligh's installation, *Sandy Ground,* is based on this free black community. To research this project, Sligh interviewed residents of the community and visited the archives of museums and libraries in Staten Island. She found oral and written histories, photographs and maps, and boxes upon boxes of information about the lives and accomplishments of African Americans who lived in Staten Island. In the artist's work, a large barn-built frame of rough, splintery timbers, suggests shelter and sanctuary. On what would have been the floor of this structure, there is a large painted map of Staten Island. Spiky, thorn laden branches are strewn around the map. Sandy Ground was a safe haven; the rest of the island was inhospitable to blacks.

A four-foot standing sculpture symbolizes the figure of Eliza Morriss Cooler, in rough, painted white plaster; it stands about where the town would be on the map. Large blue text panels with bold brush strokes offer the facts

of Cooler's life in short, dispassionate sentences. Cyanotype photographs of Sandy Ground scenes (boats, oyster fishing and the Rossville A.M.E. Zion Church) provide factual information, but every other ingredient in the piece charts emotional terrain and tells a poignant story of survival and loss.

Questions and statements like "Am I safe?" "I remember somebody" and "I don't know how to swim" isolated on one wall, resonate in this context. The swimming refers to Cooler's husband, who drowned in 1832. This haunting installation is wonderfully researched and constructed. Philip Cooler's shouts as he drowns suggest the voices of Africans who did not survive the Middle Passage. The prints are referential yet directed.

Kellie Jones points out that "Sligh [uses family snapshots] to weave narratives and fables of her/a family. Sligh's interest in recording her own reality (as distinct from that supplied by the media or by the white, male, megalomaniacal power structure of Wall Street, where she worked as a financial analyst for ten years) first led her from documentary work to her family photos. But in these as well she found only fictive poses that did not convey her history as she remembered it. By collaging and marking the images, wrapping them in her own incantations, she reinvents herself in her own image. Using cyanotype and kallitype processes, Sligh preserves the old look of her family photographs while her practice of *cliche-verre* and other forms of directorial manipulation insist on the works' contemporaneity."[13]

In *What's Happening With Momma,* Sligh creates an artist's book from her photographic diaries by restaging personal childhood and adult experiences. In the book, she tells a story as she sits on the steps with her older brother. The story becomes a mystery story about their mother who is in labor. Laura Marks observes that "Sligh's working process is more like therapy than like the process of creating an artifact. . . . Sligh uses photography as a means of self-examination and self-healing. But her art does more than that; it also examines and heals the cultural body."[14]

Margaret Stratton

examines the socialized behavioral patterns of the middle-class American family and how her family, in particular, is placed within this structure. Stratton exposes how women—mothers and daughters—collect, wear, use, preserve and display objects. She provides us with a biographical record of a way of life, describes a time through which an individual lived, and tells a story about self. Stratton becomes a voyeur in her mother's house and identifies the consumptive behavioral patterns of her mother, in particular, and of women, in general. A house sprinkled with artifacts from Western culture becomes a

signifier for identifying femininity and domesticity. Bonds that tie us to time and family are the underlying theme in her series titled *Inventory of My Mother's House.* In a straight-forward manner, Stratton explores the relationship between commonplace objects and the space the occupy in our memories. bell hooks has written of an experience akin to Stratton's: "Objects are not without spirit. As living things they touch us in unimagined ways. On this path one learns that an entire room is a space to be created, a space that can reflect beauty, peace, and a harmony of being, a spiritual aesthetic. Each space is a sanctuary."[15]

Stratton's mother, now deceased, lives forever in her memory because of these objects. What we, as strangers, began to accept in viewing this work is what we bring to it from our own personal experiences. We bring our knowledge of childhood and shared family memorabilia. The message that Stratton imparts is the affirmation of who we are and where we have been. Stratton allows us to reexamine, restage and scrutinize our family and familial traditions. The ordering and rearranging of the objects breaks up the sense of placement and utility. The presentation records humanity whether romantic or vain; it celebrates the ordinary and acknowledges humility. According to Stratton, this series is a photographic installation of 75 prints of actual objects in her parents' house:

As a group these photographs reflect the good life as well as the ease with which they slide into obsolescence—a treasure hunt of post industrial kitsch. These images also testify that what mass production has given us is an effluvia of products with either little or questionable value—things for their own sake—objects whose function is emotional rather than physical: mantles of collectibles and Franklin Furnace statuary that stand for the 'authentic'.

In some ways my parents' house is a true post-modern space, an organic and unintentional evolution from necessity to ornament that mirrors both their economic status and the robust wealth of an economy included toward the production of trifles. Within its four walls all eras and styles are represented with equal weight. Nothing is more important than anything else so nothing can be, or ever is, thrown away.

This collection of discardables, impossible to discard, is also part of my childhood; each object is infused with memories of houses long ago abandoned, and rooms irretrievably redecorated. As for the process of cataloguing, each room and its use is encoded with hierarchy: domains which reside within a social program of gendered domesticity. While some objects are undeniably my father's, others are incontestably my mother's and when photographed and placed together, begin to create a narrative that describes more than individual lives encompassing the post war America of utopian nuclear families free to consume, but not to question what it is they are buying or why.

Diane Tani

creates photo-text pieces about the Asian American experience. Her work focuses on the strengths of a collective memory of love and support as well as the unjoyous experiences of exploitation and domination within the Asian American community. Tani's work, like that of many in this exhibition, incorporates text, images from advertising, film, and television, family snapshots, and archival photographs. She focuses on pride and optimism and, at the same time, candidly exposes bigotry and oppression.

Tani states that the term Asian American grew out of the anger and refusal to let others "call us names. The term is full of history, pride (not shame), determination (not fear), and awareness (not contempt). It is a term of self-definition." The photographic sculpture titled *Bad Words* incorporates stereotypical labels coupled with images in a manner that speaks to the negativity and adversity of such oppression. This image is printed as a negative with the face of an Asian American woman behind bars with text. *Forever Foreign* is best described with the words by Kimiko Hahn:

No, I said to the man in a bar, I'm not from Saigon. Not only are Asian Americans still regarded as alien, but the women are compared to and often treated like the prostitutes "our boys" left behind in Vietnam, Korea, and Japan. Furthermore, the way American society regards us linked to each and every new wave of immigrants: then heavily Chinese and Japanese and now more Korean, Filipino, and Southeast Asian. We are the 'model minority' on the one hand and the 'dog eater' on the other. We are forever foreign.

Stereotype, is a chromogenic print derived from a television monitor. The text reads, "The term Oriental may not seem derogatory but the public had a long time to associate it with a multitude of stereotypes—Charlie Chan, Suzy Wong, Madame Butterfly." Rupert Jenkins and Chris Johnson note that "Diane Tani's photo-text pieces resonate with the ambiguities of optimism and frustration felt by many immigrants to the West. Her works bring to the surface some of the injustices which exist towards Asian Americans."[16] The artist echoes this sentiment when she says, "My grandparents—on my father's side—had come over from Japan. When Pearl Harbor happened, tensions against Japanese Americans increased and my grandmother became very nervous, and burned almost all the family snapshots."[17]

Tani's work reveals an interesting and valuable insight into the lives of Asian Americans. In documenting her personal and communal history, Tani forces the viewer to decode words and phrases often used to stereotype Asian Americans. In representing her "self-identity", she reveals the personal and societal impressions of her community and the way language is used to convey and substantiate those impressions. The titles of her work create a new contemporary lexicon and cause a re-reading of works such as *Loyalty, Gatecrasher, Boiled in the Melting Pot,* and *Appearances.*

Christian Walker

incorporates family snapshots within his own contemporary images. He reprints them with superimposed images of reproductions of Madonna and Child and paints over the surface with raw pigments. Kellie Jones notes that "[i]n his series, *Bargaining with the Dead,* Christian Walker uses the format of the family photo album to "document" a history of the extended or archetypal African American family. He enlarges this form with paint and pigment as well as vintage re-photographed images, manipulation which for him emphasizes the artistic rather than the technical aspects of the medium. At the center of Walker's fictive dramas are his own kin whose lives also fit the paradigm of fortitude vs. physical change, and embody the fragile nature of life."[18]

Through his compositions and formal manipulations, Walker examines social structures in the family. Here, he describes *Bargaining With the Dead:*

It concerns the charged emotions surrounding the deaths of my parents in 1985. It is a photo album of sorts, of the extended black family. . . . The central images follow my mother from age 19 to 55, yet they are larger, in the sense that they comment on the journey of a black woman through life. Each photograph of her, not only shows her physical changes and the depth of her struggle, these images also reveal her strength and fortitude.[19]

This is a series of biographical family photos, inspired by

grief and the death of both of his parents. Walker's family portraits and art historical images (e.g.: Gothic Madonnas) evoke the artist's own family ties and the exclusion of African-American and African imagery—thus "culture"—from the historical record. He imposes social meanings on a personal and emotional history. This brings Walker's meditations on race and society into his own biographical experience.[20]

Carrie Mae Weems

is a photographer well-known for her photographic series of family pictures; installation art; iconographic pieces on glass, ceramic, and fabric; as well as her socio-psychological depictions of race through documentary re-enactment of stereotypical subject matter. Weems's photographs are skillfully revealing. She is a compassionate storyteller who is involved with the matrix of family stories. Most of her work records or reflects social and cultural aspects of the African American family experience. Some of her most distinctive works are her *Kitchen Table* series. The kitchen table is, for many of us, the spiritual place for open discussion. Many of us gravitate to the kitchen when we smell baked and fried foods. The kitchen table is a place where one finds comfort after a difficult day at work or school; where children spread their school books; where card and chess players con-

vene. Topics discussed range from healing family strife to sharing family folklore.

Weems is an artist who weaves stories from the kitchen table to remind us how home, family, and environment become collaborative partners in the art process. The *Kitchen Table* series has a set of 20 images. The mother/daughter photographic tableaux (seen in this exhibition) are particularly intriguing. The text and images explore a relationship that is central to the family structure. Weems presents a fictive narrative and explores the complexity within various relationships: man to woman, woman to woman, woman to child, and woman alone. Susan Fisher Sterling writes of the entire series: "Weems invites us to construct a woman's story through her social relations to her man, their child, and her friends, within a setting of domestic ordinariness. The photographs are presented in chapters, each of which contains several images. The first photo "chapter" speaks between the woman and the man; the second presents the woman seeking consolation from friends and family; the third describes the woman's role as mother; and the fourth depicts the woman coping with being alone."[21]

Andrea Kirsch further critiques the series: "Weems creates a narrative work that examines the life of a woman. Each gesture, stance, and object identifies the emotional content of the moment. The narrative proceeds through a space that is fixed rigidly in three dimensions by the immobile position of the camera/photographer/ viewer which defines the spacial breadth; by the receding table; and by the prominent verticality of the overhead light." The heroine, as well as the characters in her life—friends, daughter, and lover—interact around a wooden kitchen tabletop. The format of the series is related to a tradition of narrative photographic fictions and the use of serial photography by conceptual artists. Each photograph captures a precise moment of the heroine's life that is reminiscent of film-stills. Weems herself is the model for the protagonist of the series. The viewer simultaneously identifies with the heroine and the photographer.[22]

Weems focuses on the experience of family and expands on that central theme with the compelling narrative and realism of her photographic expression.

Pat Ward Williams'

work is based on old family snapshots and experiences that have affected her as the mother of a teenage daughter. The large scale image in this exhibition is based on reconstructed photographs from the family album and computer generated images. The text includes re-lived and reconsidered thoughts about the discussions she has with her own daughter. Snapshots are mounted on the

enlarged photograph. The coded messages allow the viewer to focus on the faces of the artist's daughter at different stages in her life. *Meditations on Discovering That I Hear My Mother When I Talk to My Daughter* is a large-dot screen mural of the artist seated under the Christmas tree with her mother. Summoning up emotions of re-lived and shared experiences with her own mother, the smaller photographs made by Williams of her own daughter are dispersed over the mural. The photographs create a subtext to the larger image exploring the current interaction between mother and daughter and the similarities of the past. Working on this computer generated image, Williams raises many fundamental issues relating to the use of family photographs and memory in her art. She states:

By examining the domain of photographic images and ideas which conform to cultural ideals and measuring that against personal and individual experiences, artists can create powerful art work using family snapshots. When the family is not our own, these photographs provoke our imagination. They invite our curiosity about the personalities and relationships but can't quite satisfy it. Unlike documentary photographs which read as "official", family snapshots are imbued with a parallel personal narrative. What type of bonus is produced when eccentric details, provided by personal and cultural histories, lodged in memory, and espoused in oral histories are used to enrich our knowledge and understanding of the historical past? When working with the photographs of our own families, personal ideals, concerns, and experiences are the issue.

What forces of suppression, deletion, altercation, or elimination could be working to conceal information? Do each of us systematically ignore or falsely construct events, places and people to neatly fit the image of who we think we are today? Through acknowledging and seeking answers to these questions, I critically construct visual images of a personal and individual reality.[23]

This larger-than-life-size photograph was taken by the artist's father, who was an avid amateur photographer. The artist and her mother smile with ease for him. As Williams juxtapose the smaller images around this idealized moment, she highlights similar moments of her life with her daughter in a somewhat chronological manner. The smaller images are well placed and comfortably acknowledge that the ideals expressed by her mother still persist. *Meditations* focuses on reflection and refers to how mothers and daughters are represented in family photographs, their encounters and how primary issues evolve from one generation to another. Fatimah Tobing Rony writes, "Williams's installation. . . . invites the viewer to contemplate the different levels of history, moving at different speeds and moments."[24]

By using the dot-screen technique, Williams forces the viewer into the role of interpreter. Curator Thelma Golden writes: "Like much of Williams' work, this installation operates on many levels. The dot-screen mural must be seen from a distance, since the image breaks up into incomprehensible dots as the viewer approaches.

The collage elements, on the other hand, require intimacy and can only be viewed at close range. The two aspects of the work cannot be experienced in tandem. Williams creates a visual mode that both draws us in and pushes us away. She controls our experience of the work by selectively focusing our view. . . . to direct attention to individual parts of the whole."[25]

The subject of **Florence Flo Oy Wong's** photographic work is the lived experience of her husband , Edward K. Wong. The series entitled *The Baby Jack Rice Story* is a memory narrative of her husband who grew up in Augusta, Georgia in the segregated South of the 1940s and 1950s. The installation includes photographic silk-screened images printed on rice sacks. The photographic portraits are images of the Wong and the Cade families, probably taken sometime in the 1930s and 1940s. With about 30 black-and-white photographs of the families, plus text and drawings, *The Baby Jack Rice Story* tells the story of Ed Wong's family and the Cades, an African American family who lived near his family home. The artist states: "During our 33 years of marriage, Ed has constantly talked of his childhood and recalled his fond memories of Cush and the late Boykin Cade. In 1993, when I was an artist-in-residence at Headlands Center for the Arts, I decided to create the "Baby Jack Rice Story" and Ed and I then collaborated on the accompanying video. To make this installation possible, we traveled to Augusta to meet with Cush and the late Alma Cade Edwards who cooperated fully with us in our research to tell the story between the Wongs and the Cades. Ed and I, since our marriage in 1961, visited Augusta several times and we initially made contact with Cush and Alma two or three years ago. Alma was so pleased that Ed remembered so much about her family. The richness of Ed's memories combined with the actual recall from Cush and Alma made it possible to create "Baby Jack". We returned to Augusta this year to visit with Cush and Alma again. Unfortunately, on the day that we flew into Atlanta, Alma was buried after dying suddenly. Boykin, Ed's childhood mentor, drowned when he was in the Army during the Korean War. . . . Continuing the use of rice, rice sacks, and hand-sewing, I visually narrate the Baby Jack Rice story. I employ photo-

realism to depict elements of the telling."

Florence Wong narrates this story from the point of view of her husband and his memories of growing up in the south within an embracing and supportive community. One is reminded of family quilts when viewing the installation. Wong is the narrator/ interviewer/artist. The handwritten text serves as decoration, as the advertising text on the rice sack superficially transforms the domesticity of the family portraits into a romantic tribute to the interactions between two families. The cultural and social subject matter in Wong's work shape the photographic installation. It is intimate and yet conveys a sense of conscious familiarity. The juxtaposed imagery imposes a personal identity on images of cultural representation. She provides an interesting comparison to the work of other artists in *Imagining Families: Images and Voices* who appropriate family images in order to critique their cultural representation.

—Deborah Willis
Curator

1. Peter Galassi, *Pleasures and Terrors of Domestic Comfort*, New York: The Museum of Modern Art, 1991, p. 11.

2. Alan D. Entin, Ph.D., "Family Icons: Photographs in Family Psychotherapy," *The Newer Therapies: A Sourcebook*, L. Abt and I. Stuart, eds., New York: Van Nostrand, 1982, p. 208–209.

3. Richard Bolton, ed., *The Contest of Meaning: Critical Histories of Photography*, Cambridge, Mass: The MIT Press, 1990, p. xii.

4. Quincy Troupe, "In the Eyes, Memory Lies," *Ancestral Dialogues: The Photographs of Albert Chong*, San Francisco: The Friends of Photography, 1994, p. 1.

5. Thelma Golden, "Albert Chong: Eye & I," *Ancestral Dialogues: The Photographs of Albert Chong*, San Francisco: The Friends of Photography, 1994.

6. Kimberly Camp, *Lonnie Graham: In a Spirit House*. Exhibition

brochure. Philadelphia: The Fabric Workshop, 1993.

7. Diana C. du Pont, *Lorie Novak*. Exhibition catalogue. Long Beach, CA: Museum of Contemporary Art, University Art Museum, California State University, 1991.

8. Lorie Novak to Diana C. du Pont, Djerassi Foundation, Woodside, California, July 1990.

9. Rene Paul Barilleaux, "A Conversation with Lorie Novak," *Projections: Photographs by Lorie Novak, 1983–1990,* Madison, WI.: Madison Art Center, 1990.

10. Deborah Willis, *Lorna Simpson*. San Francisco: Friends of Photography, 1993, p. 6.

11. Ibid., p. 60.

12. Coco Fusco, "Uncanny Dissonance: The Work of Lorna Simpson," *Lorna Simpson*. Exhibition catalogue. Hamilton, NY: Cole University, Dana Arts Center, 1991.

13. Kellie Jones, "In Their Own Image," *ArtForum*, November 1990, p. 136.

14. Laura U. Marks, "Healing the Cultural Body," *Photography Center Quarterly* #50, 1991.

15. bell hooks, *Yearning: Race, Gender and Cultural Politics*, Boston: South End Press, 1990, p. 104.

16. Rupert Jenkins and Chris Johnson, "Disputed Identities: Photography," *SF Camerawork Quarterly*, Vol. 17, No. 3 (Fall 1990), p. 6.

17. Moira Roth, "Interview with Diane Tani," . . . *Crashing the Gate:*

Photographic Works by Diane Tani, Davis, CA: C.N. Gorman Museum, University of California, 1994.

18. Kellie Jones, "Towards A Visible/Visual History," *Constructed Images: New Photography*, New York: Schomburg Center for Research in Black Culture, 1989, p. 9.

19. Christian Walker, "Bargaining With the Dead," *Constructed Images: New Photography*, New York: Schomburg Center for Research in Black Culture, 1989, p. 23.

20. Glen Harper, *Christian Walker*. Exhibition brochure. Atlanta: Jane Jackson Gallery, 1992.

21. Susan Fisher Sterling, "Signifying: Photographs and Texts in the Work of Carrie Mae Weems," *Carrie Mae Weems*, Washington, DC: The National Museum of Women in the Arts, 1993, pp. 26–27.

22. Andrea Kirsch, "Carrie Mae Weems: Issues in Black, White and Color," *Carrie Mae Weems*, Washington, DC: The National Museum of Women in the Arts, 1993, pp. 14–15.

23. Pat Ward Williams, unpublished statement, 1993.

24. Fatimah Tobing Rony, "We Must First See Ourselves: Documentary Subversions in Contemporary African American Women's Photography," *Personal Narratives: Women Photographers of Color*, Winston-Salem, NC: Southeastern Center for Contemporary Photography, 1993, p. 14.

25. Thelma Golden, *Pat Ward Williams: I Remember It Well*. Exhibition brochure. Northampton, MA: Smith College Museum of Art, 1993.

Albert Chong

My ancestral dialogues are a constant discourse with the spirits of the past, and a daily improvisation of my present life. Overall, this work is an attempt to fuse the practices inherent in the cosmological system of my life with the art making process. To eliminate the distinction between art and life, ritual, magic and my own brand of personal mysticism. To bring them the ancestral spirits, and seat them on the thrones that have been created for them, upon and about which offerings are made to them.

The Throne Series are found chairs that are embellished and dedicated to ancestral and other spirit forces. Offerings of food, drink and objects that are culturally or spiritually infused are offered upon or around the thrones that are meant to attract or seat the deities.

Born
1958   Kingston, Jamaica.

Resides In
Boulder, CO.

Education
1991   M.F.A., University of California, San Diego, CA.

1981   B.F.A., Honors, School of Visual Arts, New York, NY.

Selected Solo Exhibitions
1994   *Albert Chong*, Sangre De Cristo Arts Center, Pueblo, CO.

Albert Chong, "Works from Ancestral Dialogues," The Friends of Photography, Ansel Adams Center for Photography, San Francisco, CA.

1993   *Albert Chong – Works*, Porter Randall Gallery, La Jolla, CA.

YIN / YANG, US / THEM, BLACK / WHITE, GOOD / BAD. An installation at the Bronx Museum of Art, Bronx, NY.

1991   *Albert Chong "Homecoming"*, New Photography Chelsea Galleries, Kingston, Jamaica.

1990   *Healing the Cross, Healing the Symbol: A Substitute Sacrifice*, An installation at The Mandeveille Annex Gallery, University of California, San Diego, CA.

Selected Group Exhibitions
1994   *The Fifth Havana Biennial*, Havana, Cuba.

1993   *The Family Seen*, SF Camerawork, San Francisco, CA.

Ancestral Spirits, El Camino College Art Gallery, Torrance, CA.

1992   *Cross Cultural Explorations*, The Atlanta College of Art Gallery, Atlanta, GA.

Parents, Museum of Contemporary Art at Wright State University Creative Arts Center, Dayton, OH.

1991   *The Pleasures and Terrors of Domestic Comfort*, Museum of Modern Art, New York, NY.

1990   *Convergence: 8 Photographers*, A traveling exhibition. Photographic Resource Center at Boston University, Boston, MA.

1989   *Constructed Images: New Photography*, Studio Museum in Harlem, New York, NY.

1987 *Rooms With A View*, B.C.A. Longwood Arts Gallery, Bronx, NY.

Selected Awards/Grants

1994 COVisions Recognition Award in the Visual Arts, Colorado Council on the Arts (CCA).

1993 Travel Grants Pilot Fund, Arts International and the National for the Arts.

1992 National Endowment for the Arts Individual Artist Fellowship (Photography).

1990 California Arts Council Individual Artist Fellowship (Photography).

Selected Public Collections

Artist of Color Collection, Univ. of Colorado at Boulder, Boulder, CO.

Schomburg Center of Research in Black Culture, New York, NY.

Allen Memorial Art Museum, Oberlin College, Oberlin, OH.

Erie Art Museum, Erie, PA.

Tampa Museum of Art, Tampa, FL.

Catskill Center for Photography, Woodstock, NY.

Museum of The National Center of Afro-American Artists Inc., Boston, MA.

Selected Bibliography

Galassi, Peter. *Pleasures and Terrors of Domestic Comfort*. New York: The Museum of Modern Art, 1991.

Read, Michael, ed. *Ancestral Dialogues, The Photographs of Albert Chong*. San Francisco: The Friends of Photography,

The Two Sisters   1994

Ansel Adams Center for Photography, 1993.

Willis-Thomas, Deborah. *An Illustrated Bio-Bibliography of Black Photographers, 1940-1988*. New York: Garland Publishing, 1989.

Fay Fairbrother

. . . . Having grown up in the South, the area of the country most blamed for racism, it was a shock to move to Oklahoma and find racism more prevalent and blatant than any area of the South where I had lived. Additionally, more and more articles regarding racial terrorism and violence appeared in the newspaper.

Brimming with resolve to work to remind people pictorially and through my art of this peculiar form of American inhumanity to man, I began a journey into another culture, a fascinating journey where black history intertwined with white history. I thoroughly researched the history of blacks before I began the work. It was the first time I felt possessed to produce art. I ordered all the Klan and lynching photographs I could find, not knowing how I could use them. I studied the history, literature, music, and art of African Americans. These initial incidents and research led to *The Shroud Series, Quilt Shroud I through IV.* This work combined research and photography, and is intended to remind people that racial hatred and discrimination exist.

The photographs of the KKK activities, posed studio portraits of black and white families, and lynched men clearly reflected a dissolution of family values and morals, Christian or otherwise. This behavior resulted in the removal of the black man from his family. Where does the democratic process go wrong when KKK meetings such as the ones illustrated result in black men hanging from trees?

Because the "family" structure was destroyed, I attempted to find one thing which represented "family" to me and to others, a common denominator. And the one item I kept returning to was the quilt. One is hard pressed to find a person who did not have a quilt during a lifetime. Research further revealed that when the dead were prepared for burial, they were often wrapped in quilts. The Amish made quilted coffin covers. And when a child is born into the Chickasaw tribe, a quilt is made for him or her. The child cherishes the quilt throughout life and is ultimately buried in the quilt.

The quilts are my own design based on traditional patterns, and kept simple in order for the photographs to speak. All of the quilts are full-sized or larger, made of 100% cotton fabric (in some cases overdyed), and photographic linen.

Born
1947   New Orleans, LA.

Resides In
Stillwater, OK.

Education
1994   Graduate School, College of Fine Arts, University of Oklahoma, Norman, OK.

1992   M.A., Art History, University of Oklahoma, Norman OK.

1990   B.A., Art History Oklahoma State University, Stillwater, OK.

Selected Exhibitions
1994   *Social Identity: A View From Within,* Center for Exploratory and Perceptual Art, Buffalo, NY.

```
03-17-95
15-02 0022

1       •0•75I
        •0•75I  TA
        •0•05I  TX

        •0•80 ST
        •1•00 CA  AI
        •0•20 CG
```

03-17-95
15-02 0022

1   0.751
0.751 M
0.051 M

0.804
1.004 M
0.206

The Shroud Series: Quilt Shroud I   1992

North of the Border, North Lake College, Irving, TX.

1993   *New Impressions: Photography in the 1990's*, Light Impressions Spectrum Gallery, Rochester, NY.

Issues of Oppression, Orange County Center for Contemporary Art, Los Angeles, CA.

1992   *Photobiographers*, Atlanta Gallery of Photography, Atlanta, GA.

Selected Awards/Grants

1992   Graduate Barnett Scholarship, University of Oklahoma, Norman, OK.

1991   Graduate Barnett Scholarship, University of Oklahoma, Norman, OK.

Selected Bibliography

Fairbrother, Fay. "Artemisia Gentileschi: A Great Artist and Businesswoman of the Baroque." *Proceedings: Fifth National Conference on Undergraduate Research*. Katherine M. Whatley, ed. Vol. 1. The University of North Carolina at Asheville Press, March 1992. Senior thesis.

The Spirit of Oklahoma: A Portrait of Oklahoma by Oklahomans, December 1992. Photograph published.

Lonnie Graham

This installation is dedicated to the notion and occurrence of spiritual manifestation. By committing myself to this work, I feel I have managed to address issues of relevance to a broader audience, by establishing a visual and tangible narrative that is not afield of the psychological, spiritual and physical experience of the viewing audience. In this way, the work becomes completely relevant. All of the viewer's senses are stimulated: sight, mind, touch, smell and auditory scenes (via sound track). This becomes far more pro-active than a photograph, a drawing or a painting. In this environmental context a wider variety of issues can be addressed with greater impact, depth and dimension. By paving this new avenue of self-expression and by attending to essential issues, home, community and spirituality, I feel I have more closely aligned myself to original and ancient artists and craftsmen in producing work that not only has particular ritualistic purpose, but serves as an integral part of daily life. Therefore, validation of this effort lies in the community it serves and the rewards reaped by those who find and recognize the level of truth and commitment in the work. This quality of integrating artifacts of common experience and daily life is evidenced in the work of ancient tribal artmakers which is a quality I wish to perpetuate and one I find that still has deep roots in the African American community and must be embraced to retain the value and depth of our culture. Esoteric and eccentric art making of other cultures tends to be exclusive rather than inclusive about its values and traditions. Not only is

it the responsibility of the artist to communicate essential issues to the community we serve, but without that communication and reciprocity the singular efforts of those artists remain without dimension or response and lack the wealth of interaction.

Born
1954   Cleveland, OH.

Resides In
Seldom Seen, PA.

Education
1984   M.F.A., San Francisco Art Institute, San Francisco, CA.

1978   B.F.A., San Francisco Art Institute, San Francisco, CA.

1977   Nova Scotia College of Art and Design, Halifax, Nova Scotia, Canada.

1976   A.S. in Specialized Technology, Certification in Design and Illustration, Ivy School of Professional Art, Pittsburgh, PA.

Selected Solo Exhibitions
1994   Harrisburg Area Community College, Harrisburg, PA.

Community College of Allegheny County, Pittsburgh, PA. An installation.

Brandywine Workshop, Philadelphia, PA.

1993   Temple University Gallery, Philadelphia, PA.

Meadville Council on the Arts, Meadville, PA.

1992   Manchester Craftmen's Guild Downtown Gallery, Pittsburgh, PA.

1991   Baltimore Clay Works, Baltimore, MD. Clay and photographic works.

Will Brown

In A Spirit House: Aunt Dora's Room   1993

1990   Hartwell Gallery, Pittsburgh, PA.

Selected Group Exhibitions

1994   Southern Alleghenies Museum of Art, Johnstown, PA.

Nexus Foundation for Today's Art, Philadelphia, PA.

Sardoni Art Gallery, Wilkes-Barre, PA.

Pennsylvania State Museum, Harrisburg, PA.

1993   Three Rivers Arts Festival, Pittsburgh, PA. Invitational Group Exhibition.

Fabric Workshop, Philadelphia, PA.

1992   Millersville University Art Gallery, Millersville, PA.

1991   Marcus Gordon Gallery, Pittsburgh, PA.

Selected Awards/Grants

1994   Martha's Vineyard Historical Society Artist-in-Residence, Martha's Vineyard, MA.

Arts International, a travel grant for artists, a joint project with the National Endowment for the Arts and Arts International funded by the PEW Charitable Trust.

1992   Fabric Workshop Artist in Residence, Philadelphia, PA.

1991   Pennsylvania Council on the Fellowship, Visual Artists Fellowship.

1990   Baltimore Clay Works Artists in Residence, Baltimore, MD.

1985   San Francisco Bay Guardian Photo Competition, First Place, Color Photography, San Francisco, CA.

1984   San Francisco Art Institute Spring Show Award, San Francisco, CA.

Selected Public Collections

New York Public Library, New York, NY.

Selected Bibliography

"Caught On Film," *Meadville Tribune*, Sept. 8, 1993.

Graham, Lonnie. "The Photo Workshop." *The Studio Potter Network*. Vol. 7, No. 1, Spring 1993.

Radke, Paul. "An Interview with Lonnie Graham." *Photo Metro Magazine*, Sept. 1986, Cover, p. 9.

Radke, Paul. "An Interview with Lonnie Graham." *Photo Metro Magazine*, Sept./Oct. 1992, p. 16.

Sozanski, Edward. "Identity Approached with a Cutting Edge and Kindly Nostalgia." *Philadelphia Inquirer*, July 2, 1993, p. 19.

David Keating

My current art practice, although largely photographic, involves mixed media, and uses text-and-image as well as strategies of appropriation. In this way, I can address specific and autobiographical concerns. My goal is partly political; I want to counter the repressive forces that would keep certain issues "private" and therefore unaddressed. Among these issues are family strife, racism, sexism, and AIDS. My other aim is contextual; I want people to see how images lead and mislead us.

Tennessee Williams once said "that Truth has a Protean nature, that its face changes in the eye of each beholder." In short stories and plays, Williams lets meaning fall between the lines. He allows his readers to draw their own conclusions. For me, the space between words and photographs can be used to similar effect. The questions I care to raise are not directly stated but fall within this gap.

Born
1962   Rye, NY.

Resides In
Albuquerque, NM.

Education
1991   M.A., Art, University of New Mexico, Albuquerque, NM.

1985   B.A., Philosophy, Yale University, New Haven, CT.

Selected Solo Exhibitions
1994   *Beloved*, Graham Gallery, Albuquerque, NM.

1992   *David Keating: Pending*, California Institute of the Arts, Santa Clarita, CA.

1991   *Edward, a photo-memoir*, John Sommers Gallery, University of New Mexico, Albuquerque, NM.

1990   *We Look at a Situation*, John Sommers Gallery, University of New Mexico, Albuquerque, NM. (Travelled to National Council on Alcoholism Conference of Affiliates, Nashville, TN; Peter Fingeston Gallery, Pace University, New York, NY.)

Selected Group Exhibitions
1993   *The Mediated Image: American Photography Since 1960*, University of New Mexico Fine Arts Museum, Albuquerque, NM.

1992   *Backtalk*, Randolph Street Gallery, Chicago, IL.

Dwellings of Introspection, San Jose Institute of Contemporary Art, San Jose, CA.

Private/Public, Betty Rymer Gallery, School of the Art Institute of Chicago, Chicago, IL.

Photobiographers, Atlanta Gallery of Photography, Atlanta, GA.

1991- *Disclosing the Myth of Family*, Betty Rymer Gallery,
1992   School of the Art Institute of Chicago, Chicago, IL.

1990   *The Chalice and the Blade*, Raw Space Gallery, Albuquerque, NM.

Awards/Grants
1992   Photographers and Friends United Against AIDS, Art Matters Inc.

Family Legend   1992

1991   Van Deren Coke Fellowship, University of New
        Mexico, Albuquerque, NM.

        Graduate Tuition Fellowship, University of New
        Mexico, Albuquerque, NM.

Selected Public Collections
University Art Museum, Albuquerque, NM.

Selected Bibliography
Artner, Alan. "Rare Unity," *Chicago Tribune*. April 9, 1992, p. 8.

Blumberg, Mark. "Behind the Family Facade," *San Jose Metro*.
June 18-24, 1992, p. 31.

Ellis, Simone. "Photographs by David Keating and Alejandro

Lopez," *Santa Fe New Mexican*, Oct. 12, 1990, pp. 6-7.

Fitzsimmons, Casey. "Turning the Tables," *Artweek*. Sept. 19,
1991, pp. 1, 11.

McLaughlin, Bonnie. "Artists as Critics," *Chicago Reader*.
Mar. 20, 1992, pp. 36-37.

Stevens, Mitchell. "A Family Affair," *New Art Examiner*. May
1992, pp. 17-21.

Weinstein, Michael. "Family Portraits," *New City*. Dec. 26,
1991.

Willis, Deborah. "Photobiographers," *Art Papers*. Vol. 16, No. 3
(May/June 1992), pp. 12-14.

Fern Logan

This work was informed by my explorations of the ways in which I, as a black woman living in the USA during the mid-twentieth century, have personally been affected by racism. I found that racism's most painful effect on me has been seeing the ways in which my children have internalized the racist ethic.

My children are the offspring of a mixed marriage, which is not unheard of in this country. I raised them with the sadly mistaken assumption that they would understand the color of a person's skin didn't matter in the real world. They could clearly see that I was black and their father was white and that we loved, married and produced two beautiful human beings. However, in my naivete, I left the education of those two beautiful human beings up to the Institution that continues, to this day, to view people of color as second-class citizens. These people are educated by others who don't look like them, know nothing of their history, and have no interest in teaching anything other than the history of the world according to Europe. My own children were educated by this same Institution that continues to oppress and deny the non-European true access to power. Ignorance of my own rich racial heritage precluded any positive reinforcement of the ethnicity of my children at an early age. I often wonder if they would have fared any better if I had known the true nature of racism during those years when their self-esteem was being built or destroyed.

Recently my daughter has been facing her ethnicity by

American Hero   1992

refusing to choose sides. She will not buy into the racist edict that "one drop of Black blood makes you Black," nor will she deny her African heritage by "passing" for White. When asked, she states that she is of mixed heritage. My son, on the other hand, has not dealt with the question, as far as I know, except by alienating himself from all those involved.

These pieces explore my feelings regarding my son's estrangement from his family.

The cyanotype and van dyke non-silver processes were used to produce the finished pieces. The original images and text were digitized on the MacIntosh computer using Adobe Photoshop and Microsoft Word software.

Born
1945   Queens, NY.

Resides In
Chicago, IL.

Education
1993   M.F.A. School of the Art Institute of Chicago, Chicago IL.

1991   B.S. University of the State of New York.

1976   Business Administration, Marymount Manhattan, New York, NY.

1963- Photography and Graphic Arts, Pratt Institute,
1965   Brooklyn, NY.

Selected Exhibition
1993   *Montage '93*, Rochester, NY.

There Is A World Through Our Eyes, Rockland Center for the Arts & Blue Hill Cultural Center, NY.

1990   *Coast to Coast: A Women of Color National Artist's Book Project*, Jamaica Arts Center, Queens, NY.

Memories in Non-Silver, Oasis Gallery, Marquette, MI.

The Artist Portrait Series, Van Pelt Library, Michigan Technological University, Houghton, MI.

1989   New York Public Library, Fordham Branch, Bronx, NY.

1988   *FOTOFEST '88 Herstory: Black Women Photographers*, Firehouse Gallery, Houston, TX.

FOTOFEST '88 Coast to Coast (Granny Book), Diverseworks, Houston, TX.

Awards/Grants
1993   Honorable mention, School of the Art Institute of Chicago M.F.A. Thesis Show.

1992   Parks, Chavez, King Teaching Fellowship, Michigan Technological University.

1987   Artist-in-Residence, State University of New York, Buffalo, NY.

1985   Grant Recipient: Sponsored Project, New York Council on the Arts.

Yaddo Fellowship.

Lynn Marshall-Linnemeier

Selected Public Collections

Elmhurst College Collection, Elmhurst, IL .

Harlem State Office Building, New York, NY.

Schomburg Center for Research in Black Culture, New York, NY.

Bellevue Hospital Center, New York, NY.

Selected Bibliography

"Contemporary Views on Racism in the Arts." *M/E/A/N/I/N/G.* #7, Spring 1990.

Moutoussamy-Ashe, Jeanne. *Viewfinders: Black Women Photographers.* New York: Dodd, Mead, 1986.

Willis-Thomas, Deborah. *Black Photographers from 1940–1988.* New York: Garland Publishing, 1989.

Woods, Paula, and Felix Liddell. *I Too Sing America: Book of Days.* New York: Workman Publishing, 1992.

Sanctuary and *Sometimes I Hear Voices* represent work from an important period in my life on both a personal and professional level.

In 1989, I began travelling to Mississippi to work on *Mississippi Self-Portrait*, a photo-documentary project which involved my copying family photographs and interviewing family members about their photo collections. I also documented the areas that I visited through my own photographs.

The little town of Mound Bayou, located in Bolivar County in the Mississippi Delta and the oldest town in the U.S. founded by ex-slaves, became a second home to me. The town's people were like family; Mr. Milburn Crowe in particular, a kindly gentleman and the town's unofficial "Keeper of History." It seemed I couldn't get enough of visiting Mound Bayou and the Delta.

In 1990, my father died. I turned to Mound Bayou and its people as well as my own family for comfort. I was welcomed with open arms. Feeling the need to express creatively, my feelings about the kindness shown to me and the importance of Mound Bayou in my life, *Sanctuary* was born—my first series combining photography, paint and narrative. This format continues.

Sometimes I Hear Voices, done about the same time, represents the incantatory state I experienced during my

Sometimes I Hear Voices   1992

encounters with families while traveling through their lives via their family albums. The people and places contained in those albums were like archetypes of my own family and my hometown, Southern Pines, NC, supporting my belief that our ancestors, through some mystical, psychical and perhaps even genetic connection, call out to us in times of trouble and joy.

Born
1954   Southern Pines, NC.

Resides In
Atlanta, GA.

Education
1990   B.F.A. in Photography, The Atlanta College of Art, Atlanta, GA.

1973-   Spelman College, Atlanta, GA.
1974

Selected Solo Exhibitions
1993   *The Annotated Topsy*, The Hughley Gallery and Objects, Atlanta, GA.

   Recent works by Lynn Marshall-Linnemeier, Diggs Gallery at Winston-Salem State University, Winston Salem, NC.

1992   *Borders of Faith*, The Hughley Gallery and Objects, Atlanta, GA.

Selected Group Exhibitions
1993   *An Image of You*, The Atlanta Photography Gallery, Atlanta, GA.

Constructions, Spelman College Fine Art Gallery, Atlanta, GA.

Contemporary Georgia Fine Art Photographers, The Museum of Arts and Sciences, Macon, GA.

Prototype: From Memphis to Peking, Detroit Repertory Theatre Gallery, Detroit, MI.

New Work by David Ivie and Lynn Marshall-Linnemeier, City Gallery at Chastain, Atlanta, GA.

Women on Fire, 800 East Gallery, Atlanta, GA.

1992   *Photographs from the Permanent Collection*, The High Museum of Art at Georgia Pacific, Atlanta, GA.

The Number: 13 Artists on the 13th, The University Gallery, Memphis State University, Memphis, TN.

Works by Southern Women, Fay Gold Gallery, Atlanta, GA.

1991   *Georgia Art—A New Generation*, Catherine Waddell Gallery at the Atlanta Historical Society, Atlanta, GA.

From the Chapel to the Tattoo Parlour—A Gathering of Angels, ArtSpace Contemporary Fine Art Gallery, Atlanta, GA.

Selected Awards/Grants
1994   Lila Wallace/Reader's Digest Arts International Fellowship.

1993   Northern Telecom New Works Fellowship.

Southern Arts Federation / National Endowment for the Arts Regional Visual Arts Fellowship in Photography.

Arts In The Atlanta Project.

1990   The Helen Seydel Scholarship awarded by The Atlanta College of Art.

1989   The Lyndhurst Foundation Young Career Prize.

Selected Public Collections
The City of Atlanta, Atlanta, GA.

The Hughley Gallery, Atlanta, GA.

The High Museum of Art, Atlanta, GA.

Selected Bibliography
Bradford, Thomasine. "Southern Expressions: Tales Untold." *Art Papers*, Jan./Feb. 1992.

Jinkner-Lloyd, Amy. "Atlanta, Lynn Marshall-Linnemeier at Hughley." *Art in America*, July 1992.

Krane, Susan and Carrie Pryzbilla. *Southern Expressions: Tales Untold*. Atlanta: The High Museum of Art, 1991.

Newton, David. "Photos Picture Life of Blacks in Old Mississippi." *The Durham Herald*, Feb. 1990.

White, Clarence D. "Lynn Marshall-Linnemeier: Borders of Faith." *Art Papers*, July/Aug. 1992.

Lorie Novak

Collected Visions is my fourth slide installation exploring the relationship of snapshots to collective memory. In my earlier pieces, I combined snapshots from my family archive with imagery from the media to create a dialogue between the personal and the cultural. In recontextualizing my family's snapshots, I have emphasized the psychological and emotional content of snapshot images and questioned how truthful these images are. What myths about memory do they reveal?

The inspiration for *Collected Visions* came from my family snapshots. I come from a family of girls—sisters, nieces, and all female cousins. As I began to think about a new slide installation about growing up female, I wanted to see my family snapshots in relation to other women's family snapshots. I had many questions. What would be revealed about the female experience? What is universal? How do girls present themselves to the camera? Who determines the stereotypes? I solicited snapshots from my friends, my students and colleagues at NYU, and members of the Houston Center for Photography (who commissioned *Collected Visions*) community. Close to 75 women generously loaned me snapshots so I was able to draw from images of approximately 100 girls and women.

The piece is divided into three segments. The large horizontal sequence that you see upon entering begins and ends with the telling of secrets between grandmother and granddaughter. As I pored over hundreds of snap-

shots, I realized that they revealed information about how girlhood is represented, and could only hint at the actual experience of coming of age. I was struck by the similarity of so many images and the universality of the poses. I became interested in subtleties of gaze and gesture that became the clues for me about how girls find their voices. In this sequence open books about women (such as *A Room of One's Own, Little Women, Nancy Drew, Talking Back, Writing A Woman's Life*) are superimposed over many of the images.

The vertical sequence adjacent to this sequence is more meditative and lyrical, but visually echoes the other two sequences. These two sequences are ten minutes long, corresponding to the length of the music. Opposing them is a corner sequence. The images are arranged chronologically by age of the subjects but not by time periods. This 20 minute sequence traces girls from age one (when toddlers learn to stand alone and are first photographed as autonomous individuals) through adolescence. As the images dissolve from wall to wall, a dialogue is created between these images. In this sequence, I was intrigued by girls' fantasies as manifested in "dress up" outfits, how they were dressed up by their parents, and then chose their own dress as they grew up, the likeness of pose and gesture, and what gesture and dress revealed about who was in control when the photograph was taken.

Elizabeth Brown's music is integral to the piece—our parts cannot exist alone. This is the first time I have commissioned an original composition for an installation piece. Elizabeth and I had wanted to collaborate since we first met, and my vision for this piece seemed perfect for

Hans Staartjes

Collected Visions 1993

her music. The emotive qualities of memory and recollection become fully realized by the synthesis of images and music.

I want to thank all the women and girls who lent me their snapshots. I was very touched by their generosity. *Collected Visions* would not have been realized without their support.

Elizabeth Brown

I met Lorie in January 1990, when we were both artists in residence at the MacDowell Colony. Lorie was projecting images onto the landscape at night, and I'd see them as I walked to my studio (we are both nocturnal). I think we felt an immediate artistic affinity—I was working on concepts of memory and resonance, and felt I could "hear" Lorie's pictures. We decided then and there to collaborate, and have witnesses and photos to prove it.

I was looking for music that would sound like something you remembered or dreamed about. I wanted it to have lots of color and motion, but be mesmerizing rather than grab attention at any one point. Also, the ten minutes of music needed to loop, so the end and beginning had to match up. I watched Lorie's sequences at various points to get a feel for the mood—*poignant* seems close. I thought about the aural equivalent of the dissolve, which in its simplest form is overlapping resonance. The music accomplishes this in several ways: the instruments themselves are very resonant (the viola *d' amore* has seven "sympathetic" strings, which make an aura above its sound, for example); the music is written with over-lapping time values; and it was recorded in a very resonate space (The Church of the Good Shepherd in Manhattan).

When Lorie and I first played music with the slide sequences, we were amazed how well they went together. We are both very painstaking workers individu-ally; putting our contributions together was almost effortless.

Born
1954   Los Angeles, CA.

Resides In
Brooklyn, NY.

Education
1979   M.F.A., School of the Art Institute of Chicago, Chicago, IL.

1975   B.A. in Art and Psychology, Stanford University, Stanford, CA.

1971- University of California, Los Angeles, CA.
1974

Selected Solo Exhibitions
1993   *Breda Fotografica*, De Beyerd Museum, Breda, The Netherlands.

       Collected Visions, Commissioned Slide Installation, Houston Center for Photography, Houston, TX.

1992   Jayne H. Baum Gallery, New York, NY.

1991   *Traces: A Site Specific Projected Installation*, Museum of Contemporary Art, Chicago, IL.

1990   *Projections, Photographs 1983-90*, Madison Art Center, Madison, WI.

       Critical Distance, Addison Gallery of American Art, Andover, MA.

Selected Group Exhibitions
1993   *flesh & blood*, Friends of Photography, San Francisco, CA.

       Fabricated Realities, The Museum of Fine Arts, Houston, TX.

Mapping: Identities, The Museum of Contemporary Photography, Chicago, IL.

Betrayal of Means / Means of Betrayal, Southeast Museum of Photography, Daytona Beach, FL.

1992   *Representatives: Women from the Permanent Collection*, Center for Creative Photography, Tucson, AZ.

The Invention of Childhood, John Michael Kohler Arts Center, Sheboygan, WI.

Parents, Museum of Contemporary Art, Wright State University, Dayton, OH.

1991   *Pleasures and Terrors of Domestic Comfort*, Museum of Modern Art, New York, NY.

1990   *Constructed Spaces*, Photographic Resource Center & Boston Architectural Center, Boston, MA.

Selected Awards/Grants

1993   Presidential Fellowship, New York University.

1990   National Endowment for the Arts Fellowship.

Residencies, Djerassi Foundation, Woodside, CA.

1990, 1987   Residencies, MacDowell Artist Colony, Peterborough, NH.

1988   New York Foundation for the Arts Fellowship.

1987   Louis Comfort Tiffany Foundation Grant.

1980-78

Polaroid Corporation Materials Grant.

Selected Public Collections

Art Institute of Chicago, Chicago, IL.

Bibliotheque Nationale, Paris, France.

Center for Creative Photography, Tucson, AZ.

International Center for Photography, New York, NY.

International Polaroid Collection, Lausanne, Switzerland.

Jewish Museum, New York, NY.

Museum of Fine Arts, Boston, MA.

Museum of Modern Art, New York, NY.

Victoria and Albert Museum, London, England.

Selected Bibliography

Ballerini, Julia, ed. *SEQUENCE(con)SEQUENCE*. New York: Aperture Foundation, 1989.

Barilleaux, Rene Paul. *Projections: Photographs by Lorie Novak 1983-1990*. Exhibition brochure. Madison, WI: Art Center, 1990.

du Pont, Diana. *Centric 42: Lorie Novak*. Exhibition brochure. Long Beach, CA: University Art Museum, California State University, 1991.

Options 43: Lorie Novak. Exhibition brochure. Chicago: Museum of Contemporary Art, 1991.

Sheldon, James. *Issues of Projection / Photographs and Installations*. Brochure. Andover, MA: Addison Gallery of American Art, 1990.

Lorna Simpson

Coiffure

The three images depict a sequence which focuses the viewer's attention from the back of a young woman's head, curly hair cropped short, to an elegant, braided "coiffure," isolated against a deep black background, to the back of an African mask which mimics the Brancusi-like circular form of the wrapped braids. Below the triptych, a series of fragmented texts give bits of instrumental information about the braiding process.

Phillip Brookman
The Corcoran Gallery of Art
Washington, DC

Born
1960   Brooklyn, NY.

Resides In
Brooklyn, NY.

Education
1985   M.F.A. in Visual Arts, University of California, San Diego, CA.

1982   B.F.A. in Photography, The School of Visual Arts, New York, NY.

Selected Solo Exhibitions
1994   *Lorna Simpson: Standing in the Water,* Whitney Museum of American Art at Phillip Morris, New York, NY.

1992   *Lorna Simpson,* Temple University, Tyler School of Art, Elkins Park, PA.

Rhona Hoffman Gallery, Chicago, IL.

1991   *Lorna Simpson,* Colgate University, The Gallery of the Department of Art and Art History, Hamilton, NY.

1990   *Perspectives 15: Lorna Simpson,* The Portland Art Museum, Portland, OR.

Lorna Simpson: Projects 23, Museum of Modern Art, New York, NY.

Centric 38: Lorna Simpson, University Art Museum, California State University, Long Beach, CA and University Art Museum, Berkeley, CA.

1989   *Lorna Simpson / Matrix 107,* Wadsworth Atheneum, Hartford, CT.

Josh Baer Gallery, New York, NY.

Selected Group Exhibitions
1992   *Somewhere Between Image and Text,* Barbara Krakow Gallery, Boston, MA.

HomeFront: Comprehending a Common Language, Falkirk Cultural Center, San Rafael, CA.

The Fortune Teller, Rochdale Art Gallery, Lancashire, England.

1991   *Word as Image: American Art 1960-1990,* Contemporary Arts Museum, Houston, TX.

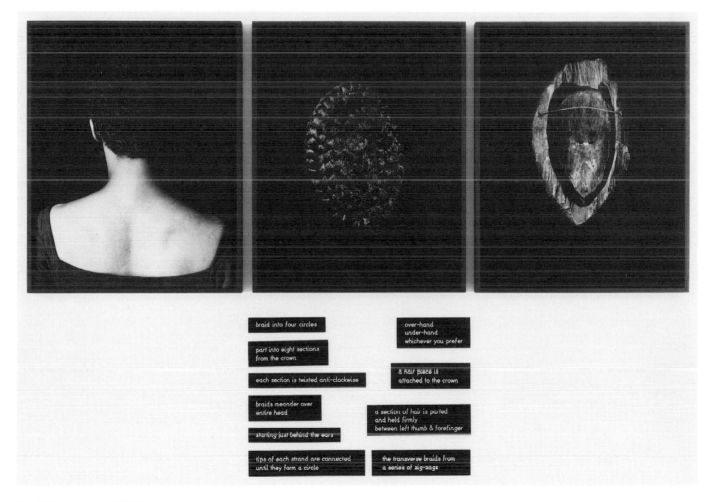

Coiffure 1991

de-Persona, The Oakland Museum, Oakland, CA.

1991 Biennial Exhibition, The Whitney Museum of American Art, New York, NY.

1990 *Aperto '90,* Venice Biennale.

The Decade Show, The New Museum of Contemporary Art, New York, NY.

Selected Awards/Grants

1994 Artist Award for Distinguished Body of Work, Exhibition, Presentation, or Performance, College Art Association, New York, NY.

1991   Distinguished Artist-in-Residence, The Christian A. Johnson Endeavor Foundation, Colgate University, Hamilton, NY.

1990   Louis Comfort Tiffany Award, Louis Comfort Tiffany Foundation, New York, NY.

Selected Public Collections
Department of Cultural Affairs, Chicago, IL.

Milwaukee Art Museum, Milwaukee, WI.

Museum of Modern Art, New York, NY.

The Brooklyn Museum, Brooklyn, NY.

The Denver Museum of Art, Denver, CO.

The High Museum of Art, Atlanta, GA.

The Corcoran Gallery of Art, Washington, DC.

Selected Bibliography
Ballerini, Julia. *The Surrogate Figure: Intercepted Identities in Contemporary Photography*. Woodstock, NY: The Center For Photography, 1991.

Fusco, Coco. "Uncanny Dissonance: The Work of Lorna Simpson." *Lorna Simpson*. Hamilton, NY: Colgate University, 1991.

Fairbrother, Trevor. *The Binational / Art of the Late 80's*. Boston: The Institute of Contemporary Art and Museum of Fine Arts, 1988.

Jones, Kellie. *Lorna Simpson*. New York: Josh Baer Gallery, 1989.

Jones, Ronald, et al. *de-Persona*. Oakland, CA: The Oakland Museum, 1991.

Ross, David and Lisa Philips. *1991 Whitney Biennial*. New York: The Whitney Museum of American Art, 1991.

Solomon-Godeau, Abigail. "Beyond the Simulation Principle," *Utopia Post Utopia: Configurations of Nature and Culture in Recent Sculpture and Photography*. Boston: Institute of Contemporary Art, 1988, pp. 83-100.

Willis, Deborah. *Lorna Simpson: Untitled Series*. San Francisco: Friends of Photography, 1992.

Wright, Beryl J. and Saidiya V. Hartman. *Lorna Simpson: For the Sake of the Viewer*. New York: Universe Publishing Inc., div. of Rizzoli International Publications, 1992.

XLIV Esposizione Internationale d'Arte La Biennale di Venezia. Venice, Italy, 1990. Catalogue.

Clarissa Sligh

My work is an attempt to connect the mind and body to the ever-present past in our continuing presence. Central to what I do is the construction and reconstruction of an image until I fully resonate with it. Images, stories, and words provide the structure for exploration. Vibrations ring quietly or discordantly or pulsate, throb, or electrify the threads of my experiences.

For *Sandy Ground,* I talked and visited with people, museums, and archives on Staten Island. I found oral and written histories, photographs and maps, and boxes upon boxes of information about the lives and accomplishments of Black Americans who lived on Staten Island.

The creation of my imagery for this project was strongly influenced by many factors. Some of them were: (1) my numerous trips on the ferry as I travelled between Manhattan and Staten Island; (2) my visit to the site of the Sandy Ground community; (3) my visit to the ship graveyard and other cemeteries on Staten Island; (4) the story of Eliza Morriss, a free black woman, who lived most her life during the enslavement of most of the blacks in this country; and (5) the migration of free black oysterman and their families from the eastern shore of Virginia and Maryland to Staten Island. I cannot describe concretely what the experience is when I work—it is very close to who I was and who I am.

Reading Dick and Jane With Me is an illustrated reader seen through the eyes of a black woman artist who spent her childhood growing up poor in the American south of the 1940s and 1950s. It is a combination of lively, repetitive words, photographs and drawings. Sligh "reads" the images of Dick and Jane and inserts words on each page, e.g.: "You play in your good clothes every page. We must keep ours nice for Sunday School days." She focuses us on the psychological effect that a primary school reader may have had on black children reading the book.

Born
Washington, DC.

Resides In
New York, NY.

Education

1979- The International Center for Photography, New York,
1980 NY.

1973 M.B.A., University of Pennsylvania, Philadelphia, PA.

1972 B.F.A., Howard University, Washington, DC.

1961 B.S., Hampton University, Hampton, VA.

Selected Solo Exhibitions

1992 Art In General, New York, NY.

The Center for Photography in Woodstock, Woodstock, NY.

1991 Light Work Menschel Gallery at Syracuse University, Syracuse, NY.

Washington Project for the Arts, Washington, DC.

1990 Meridian Gallery, San Francisco, CA.

Manchester Craftsmen's Guild, Pittsburgh, PA.

Selected Group Exhibitions

1994 *History 101: The Re-Search for Family.* Forum for Contemporary Art, St. Louis, MO.

1992 *Malcolm X: Man, Ideal, Icon.* A traveling exhibition. Walker Art Center, Minneapolis, MN.

Personal Scenarios, The Light Factory, Charlotte, NC.

The Presence of the Past, Newhouse Center for Contemporary Art, Snug Harbor Cultural Center, Staten Island, NY.

Bridges & Boundaries: African Americans and American Jews. A traveling exhibition. The Jewish Museum, New York, NY.

1991 *Recent Acquisitions: Prints and Drawings,* The Museum of Modern Art, New York, NY.

Photographic Book Art in the United States, A travelling exhibition, The University of Texas at San Antonio Art Gallery, San Antonio, TX.

1990 *Convergence: 8 Photographers,* A traveling exhibition. Photographic Resource Center at Boston University, Boston, MA.

Selected Awards/Grants

1994 Jerome Foundation Grant for Leadership Workshop, Minneapolis, MN.

1992 Artiste en France.

1990 New York State Council on the Arts Visual Artists Sponsored Work Project Award.

1988 National Endowment for the Arts.

New York Foundation for the Arts.

Selected Public Collections

The Museum of Modern Art, New York, NY.

Australian National Gallery, Canberra, Australia.

The National Museum of Women in the Arts, Washington, DC.

The Schomburg Center for Research in Black Culture, The New York Public Library, New York, NY.

The University of Arizona, Tucson, AZ.

Dartmouth College, Hanover, NH.

Selected Bibliography

Bridges & Boundaries: African Americans and American Jews. New York: The Jewish Museum at The New York Historical Society, 1992.

Hoone, Jeffrey. *Clarissa Sligh: The Presence of Memory.* Syracuse, NY: Robert B. Menschel Photography Gallery, Syracuse University, 1991.

Lippard, Lucy and Mel Watkin. *History 101: The Re-Search for*

Ellen Eisenran

Sandy Ground   1992–1994

Family. St. Louis, MO: Forum for Contemporary Art, 1994.

Marks, Laura U. "Healing the Cultural Body: Clarissa Sligh's Unfinished Business," *Photography Center Quarterly.* No. 50, 1992, pp. 18–22.

Moore, Robin and Alan Prokop. *Clarissa Sligh Witness to Dis-* *sent: Remembrance and Struggle.* Installation brochure. Washington, DC: Washington Project for the Arts, 1991.

Roth, Moira. *Personal Odysseys: The Photography of Celia Alvarez Munoz, Clarissa T. Sligh, and Maria Martinez-Canas.* Traveling exhibition catalogue. New York: Intar Gallery, 1989.

Margaret Stratton

The work in this exhibition crosses from the province of the family, the home and the private, into public arenas where cycles of consumption, rejection, the garage sale, the flea market, the attic, Goodwill and the Salvation Army all play parts in the circulation of goods into and out of the family home.

In any home, objects that dictate hierarchies of good and bad taste, fashionable trends, marketing strategies, and priceless heirlooms accumulate and co-exist within the domestic scene, sometimes side-by-side. Rooms themselves are created to house certain objects in a context that makes them presentable. The den, the guest room, the recreation room (or "rec-room" as my parents called it), the basement and, of course, the living room, all invite a selection and placement of objects that concur with the ways we think about and even behave in those rooms.

When I was growing up, my mother worked hard to create not simply a home, but a setting for what she believed would reveal her worth, her station, even her aspirations. For many years, she decorated, arranged, and rearranged the enormous brick house my parents bought in 1963, eventually almost doubling its size. She did all of the design work herself, making the house into a place as individual as she. She installed shocking mustard countertops in the kitchen; in the bathroom went seashell-shaped sinks of marble, illuminated by rows of lights like you see in actors' dressing rooms. The family room contained a two-story flagstone fireplace my father decorated with little plastic toys as far as he could reach. There was a matching "plant-box" made of the same rugged stone that looked alarmingly coffin-like, and which the cat invariably used as a sandbox.

Walls were torn down, staircases moved from one part of the house to another. There was a period of time when I was about 12 when the only access to the upstairs was a ladder you climbed to the second story, entering the bedrooms through Mother's walk-in cedar closet. The upstairs bathroom was done entirely in pink, complete with sweeping violet curtains arranged over a pink bathtub, and wild fuchsia and pink formica floor; a large furry pink stool shaped like a mushroom completed the room. In short, my childhood home was visual bedlam.

Every time I came home from camp, or vacation, and later from college, she had done something else to the house. Once my bedroom was redone entirely in yellow, with long wormy-looking shag carpeting of yellow and orange that I was forced to live with for the next 10 years. Mother loved to shop and she couldn't throw anything away. The house was a time capsule; it was also an embarrassment. When she bought gold-plated toilet handles for the downstairs bathroom, I was mortified. All my friends trooped over; they had to see it to believe it. I did get enormous sympathy from everyone.

The objects you see represented here are from my

Inventory of My Mother's House   1990–1991

mother's collection, and are also a symbolic representation of the house I grew up in. Placing these objects on black and photographing them out of the context of the house is meant as much to insinuate scrutiny as it is to imply value. The formality of the images themselves are in counterpoint to the objects presented. There is only one person physically represented in the work; it is me, in a childhood photograph. In some ways I believe I was as much a part of my mother's relentless collecting as the things she found so dear. She died three months after the work was shown, but I was fortunate to have her attend the first opening. Both of my parents were honored by the work, and proud of me, and I realized I inherited both a predilection for loving a plethora of objects, as well as a good sense of humor from them both.

Born
1953   Seattle, WA.

Resides In
Iowa City, IA.   Chicago, IL.

Education
1986   M.F.A., Art, University of New Mexico, Albuquerque, NM.

1983   M.A., Art, University of New Mexico, Albuquerque, NM.

1977   B.A., Art, Evergreen State College, Olympia, WA.

Selected Solo Exhibitions
1991   *A Post-Apocalyptic Dictionary,* Cornish College of the Arts, Seattle, WA.

In the Shadow of the Blast, Intermedia Arts Gallery, Minneapolis, MN.

1990   *After the Holocaust—A Post Nuclear Installation,* College of the Pacific, Stockton, CA. Collaboration with Jacqueline English.

1988   *Television Celebrities,* New Works Gallery, University of Illinois, Chicago, IL.

Selected Group Exhibitions
1993   *The Nuclear Club,* Gallery of New South Wales, Sydney, Australia.

1992   *Ann Hamilton/Margaret Stratton,* Henry Gallery, University of Washington, Seattle, WA.

Memories of Home, Port Angeles Fine Arts Center, Port Angeles, WA.

1991   *Critical Reactions,* Rena Bransten Gallery, San Francisco, CA.

Moving Light: Seeing and Believing, John Michael Kohler Art Center, Sheboygan, WI.

1990   *Positive Actions Visual AIDS Competition,* DC 37 Gallery, New York, NY.

1989   *Serious Fun, Truthful Lies,* Randolph Street Gallery, Chicago, IL.

The Alternative Image, NAME Gallery, Chicago, IL. Video screening.

Image/TV, Arts Center Gallery, College of DuPage, Glen Ellyn, IL.

Awards/Grants
1991   Artists 1990 Public Works Project, Seattle Arts Commission, Seattle, WA.

1990   National Endowment for the Arts Individual Fellowship in Photography, Washington, DC.

1988   National Endowment for the Arts/Rockefeller Foundation Interdisciplinary Arts Award, Intermedia Arts, Minneapolis, MN.

1987   National Endowment for the Arts Regional Visual Fellowship Award, Arts Midwest, Minneapolis, MN.

Selected Public Collections
First Bank of Minneapolis, MN.

Seattle Arts Commission, Seattle, WA.

Video Data Bank, Chicago, IL.

Women Make Movies, New York, NY.

University of Iowa Museum of Art, Iowa City, IA.

University of New Mexico Museum of Art, Albuquerque, NM.

Evergreen State College Library, Olympia, WA.

Center for Photography Northwest, Seattle, WA.

Bishop Museum, Honolulu, HI.

Selected Bibliography
"Art Addresses Life In Exhibit," *Daily Lobo* (Albuquerque, NM), Dec. 14, 1984.

Backus, Charles. "Phinney Center Exhibition," *Northwest Photo Network* (Seattle, WA), Aug. 1988, p. 12.

Baker, Kenneth. "Critical Reactions at Rena Bransten," *San Francisco Chronicle,* April 29, 1991.

Maschal, Richard. "Manipulated Photos Dominate Show," *Charlotte Observer*, April 14, 1985, p. 14.

McCracken, David. "Exhibit Has Its Fun and Its Serious Sides," *Chicago Tribune,* March 10, 1989, sec. 7, p. 56.

Diane Tani

This current body of work is part of a continuing series concerned with raising issues that have been concealed and integrated into our society. I question the image and identity of Asian Americans, specifically, and the acceptance of these portrayals, generally. I wish to attack stereotypes and the complacent acceptance of them. My aim is to bring these problems to the surface in hopes of rousing attention to these disguised impediments.

This series has evolved from reinterpreting history to confronting concealment. Often history is presented with nostalgia and a romantic reinterpretation. In this act of romanticizing, the atrocities are cleaned and polished. Through my work, I wish to deconstruct the images that the media uses to manipulate our perceptions.

Around 1988, I moved away from my earlier small format photo sculptures to 16″ x 20″ chromogenic photographs. The size shift allows the pieces to communicate to a larger group of people at one time and, hopefully, also assumes the effect of a proclamation. The images continue to be culled from a variety of sources—the media, family photographs, and archives. All of these images have shaped the perception of Asian Americans and relay messages of their own. I started to use text because many of the sentiments I am addressing are verbal as well as visual. The language comes both from offensive media messages and family sayings.

My work had developed from the personal and explanatory to the public and provoking. It is no longer sufficient to define myself, alone and isolated. It is important to recognize the circumstances in which we all live and interact. My goal is to examine and discuss, rather than to place blame. It is through these dialogues that a solution may be found. In order to advance, we must understand one another.

Born
1965   San Francisco, CA.

Resides In
San Francisco, CA.

Education
1990   M.F.A., Fine Arts/Photography, University of New Mexico, Albuquerque, NM.

1988   B.A., Art/Photography, Minor in Asian American Studies, San Francisco State University, San Francisco, CA.

Selected Exhibitions
1995   *Family Matters,* Atlanta College of Art, Atlanta, GA.

1994   *The Visual Diary,* Houston Center for Photography, Houston, TX.

1993   *Redefining Self: Six Asian American Artists,* San Jose State University, San Jose, CA.

1992   *Do You See What I See?,* College of Marin, Kentfield, CA.

Women's Work, commissioned public art project addressing domestic violence, funded and supported by Liz Claiborne, Inc. Bus shelters and billboards in San Francisco and Oakland, CA.

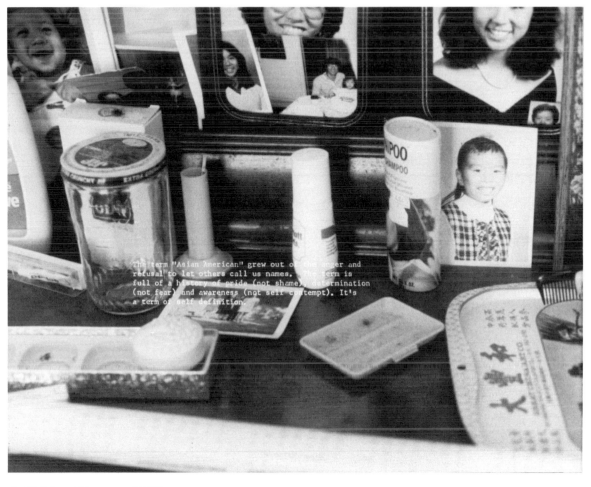

The term "Asian American" grew out of the anger and refusal to let others call us names. The term is full of a history of pride (not shame), determination (not fear) and awareness (not self contempt). It's a term of self definition.

Self-Identity 1989

HomeFront: Comprehending a Common Language, Falkirk Cultural Center, San Rafael, CA.

Gathering, Asian American Women Artists Association, Lite Rail Gallery, Sacramento, CA.

1991 *Pleasures and Terrors of Domestic Comfort,* A traveling
1993 exhibition. Museum of Modern Art, New York, NY.

1991 *Spirit of East and West,* Asian American Women Artists Association, Berkeley Store Gallery, Berkeley, CA and Chinatown Community Arts Gallery, San Francisco, CA.

New Bay Area Photographers, San Francisco State University Art Department, San Francisco, CA.

Christian Walker

1990   *Disputed Identities,* U.K. / U.S.A. traveling exhibition. SF Camerawork, San Francisco, CA.

Selected Awards/Grants

1992   *Women's Work,* commissioned public art project addressing domestic violence.

1991   Eureka Fellowship, Fleishhacker Foundation, San Francisco, CA.

1989   Honorable Mention, Bay Guardian Photo Contest, San Francisco, CA.

Selected Bibliography

Baker, Michelle. "Another Side of Photography." *Artweek,* April 30, 1988, pp. 1, 11.

Bonetti, David. "Artist Explores 'Otherness'." *San Francisco Examiner* Nov. 2, 1990, pp. C-2.

Hiura, Barbara. "Artist Joins Fight Against Domestic Violence." *Hokubei Mainichi,* Sept. 15, 1992, p. 1.

Kano, Betty and Elaine Kim, eds. *Visions and Fierce Dreams: The Lives and Works of Asian American Artists.* Philadelphia: Temple University Press, 1994.

Okutsu, James K., ed. *Fusion 6: A Japanese American Anthology.* San Francisco: Asian American Studies Department, San Francisco State University, 1990, pp. 49-57.

Redefining Self: Six Asian American Artists. San Jose, CA: San Jose State University, 1993.

SF Camerawork Quarterly. Rupert Jenkins, ed. Winter 1990.

Bargaining With The Dead. It concerns the charged emotions surrounding the deaths of my parents in 1985. It is a photo album of sorts, of the extended black family. Using old family photographs, new images, fine art reproductions, paint and raw pigments, these images speak about the fragile nature of life. The central images follow my mother from age 19 to 55, yet they are larger, in the sense that they comment on the journey of a black woman through life. Each photograph of her, not only shows her physical changes and the depth of her struggle, these images also reveal her strength and fortitude.

Born
1954   Springfield, MA.

Resides In
Atlanta, GA.

Education
1983   Fine Arts Diploma, Photography/Film, School of the Museum of Fine Arts, Boston, MA.

Selected Group Exhibitions
1992   *Subject/Object, Photographs 1980-1992,* Nexus Contemporary Art Center, Atlanta, GA.

Mule Tales, Jackson Fine Art, Atlanta, GA.

Back Home, Reflections of African American Communities: Photographs from the High Museum of Art Collection, High Museum of Art, Atlanta, GA.

Bargaining with the Dead: Great Grandmother, Uncles, Aunt   1986–1988

1991 *No More Hero's: Unveiling Masculinity,* SF Camerawork, San Francisco, CA.

1990 *The Decade Show,* Museum of Contemporary Hispanic Art, Museum of Contemporary Art, The Studio Museum of Harlem, New York, NY.

Convergence: Eight Photographers, The Photographic Resource Center, Boston, MA.

1989 *Constructed Images: New Photography,* The Studio Museum of Harlem, New York, NY.

Black Photographers Bear Witness: One Hundred Years

Carrie Mae Weems

of Social Protest, Williams College Museum of Art, Willliamstown, MA.

Selected Public Collections
Center for Creative Photography, Tucson, AZ.

High Museum of Art, Atlanta, GA.

Museum of Fine Arts, Houston, TX.

Selected Bibliography
Fox, Catherine. "A Collaboration of Artistry/Pain: AIDS Art Action Hits Home Hard." *Atlanta Journal/Constitution,* Jan. 19, 1990, p. D2.

Grundberg, Andy. "A Century of Black History Brought In Focus." *New York Times,* July 2, 1989, p. 26.

Hagen, Charles. "How Racial and Cultural Differences Affect Art." *New York Times,* Aug. 23, 1991, p. C5.

Walker, Christian. "The Miscegenated Gaze." *SF Camerawork Quarterly,* Summer 1991.

_____. *The Theatre Project.* Kirkland, WA: Nexus Press, 1985. 28 duotone photographs.

Born
1953   Portland, OR.

Resides In
Oakland, CA.

Education
1984-   Graduate Program, African American Folklore, Univer-
1987   sity of California, Berkeley, CA.

1984   M.F.A., University of California, San Diego, CA.

1981   B.A., California Institute of the Arts, Valencia, CA.

Selected Solo Exhibitions
1993   *Carrie Mae Weems: Recent Works,* P.P.O.W., New York, NY.

   Carrie Mae Weems, National Museum of Women in the Arts, Washington, DC.

1992   *And 22 Million Very Tired and Very Angry People,* Walter/McBean Gallery, San Francisco Art Institute, San Francisco, CA.

   Installation, Nexus Gallery, Atlanta, GA.

   Family Pictures and Stories, Cleveland Center for Contemporary Art, Cleveland, OH.

1991   *Currents: Carrie Mae Weems,* Institute of Contemporary Art, Boston, MA.

   Carrie Mae Weems/MATRIX 115, Wadsworth Atheneum, Hartford, CT.

Untitled (Woman with Daughter) 1990

1990 *Carrie Mae Weems,* CEPA Gallery, Buffalo, NY.

Selected Group Exhibitions
1994 *Equal Rights and Justice,* High Museum of Art, Atlanta, GA.

1993 *Personal Narratives: Women Photographers of Color,* Southeastern Center for Contemporary Art, Winston-Salem, NC.

1992 *Disclosing the Myth of Family,* Betty Rymer Gallery, School of the Art Institute of Chicago, Chicago, IL.

Mistaken Identities, University Art Museum, University of California, Santa Barbara, CA.

Fictions of the Self: The Portrait in Contemporary Photography, University Gallery, University of Massachusetts at Amherst, MA.

Dirt and Domesticity: Construction of the Feminine, Whitney Museum of Art at Equitable Center, New York, NY.

1991 *Reframing the Family,* Artists Space, New York, NY.

Carrie Mae Weems and Jeffrey Hoone, Camerawork, London, England.

Sexuality, Image and Control, Houston Center for Photography, Houston, TX.

Pleasures and Terrors of Domestic Comfort, Museum of Modern Art, New York, NY.

Outspoken Women, Intermedia Arts, Minneapolis, MN.

1990 *Who Counts?* Randolph Street Gallery, Chicago, IL.

The Race: Do We Get There At The Same Time? School 33 Art Center, Baltimore, MD.

Disputed Identities, SF Camerawork, San Francisco, CA.

1989 *Black Photographers Bear Witness: 100 Years of Social Protest,* Williams College Museum of Art,

Williamstown, MA.

Prisoners of Image: Ethnic and Gender Stereotypes, Alternative Museum, New York, NY.

Selected Awards/Grants

1992   Louis Comfort Tiffany Award.

1990   Artist in Residence, Art Institute of Chicago, Chicago, IL.

1989-   Artist in Residence, Rhode Island School of Design, 1990   Providence, RI.

1988   Artist in Residence, Light Work, Syracuse, NY.

        Massachusetts Artists Fellowship.

1987   Smithsonian Institution Fellow.

Selected Bibliography

And 22 Million Very Tired and Very Angry People. Catalogue. San Francisco: Walter/McBean Gallery, San Francisco Art Institute, 1992.

The Art of Advocacy. Catalogue. Ridgefield, CT: The Aldrich Museum, 1991.

"Disputed Identities." *SF Camerawork Quarterly,* Fall 1990.

Kirsh, Andrea, and Susan Fisher Sterling. *Carrie Mae Weems,* Exhibition catalogue. Washington, DC: The National Museum of Women in the Arts, 1993.

Parents. Catalogue. Dayton, OH: Dayton Art Institute, Museum of Contemporary Art at Wright State University, Creative Arts Center, 1992.

A Portrait is not a Likeness. Catalogue. Tucson, AZ: Center for Creative Photography, University of Arizona, 1991.

Signs of the Self: Changing Perceptions. Catalogue. Woodstock, NY: Woodstock Artists Association, 1990.

States of Loss: Migration, Displacement, Colonialism, and Power. Catalogue. Jersey City Museum, 1993.

Then What? Photographers and Folklore. Catalogue. Buffalo, NY: CEPA Gallery, 1990.

Wilson, Judith, and Andrea Miller Keller. *Carrie Mae Weems/Matrix 115.* Hartford, CT: The Wadsworth Atheneum, 1991.

Pat Ward Williams

Born
1948   Philadelphia, PA.

Resides In
Venice, CA.

Education
1987   M.F.A., Photography, Maryland Institute of Art, Baltimore, MD.

1982   B.F.A., Photography, Moore College of Art and Design, Philadelphia, PA.

Selected Solo Exhibitions
1994   *Be Black or Die (things to do),* P.P.O.W., New York, NY.

      Deuce of Clubs, Camerawork, San Francisco, CA.

1993   *I Remember It Well,* Smith College, Northampton, MA.

      Racial Politics 101, Camerawork, San Francisco, CA.

1992   *Vantage Point,* Santa Monica Museum of Art, Santa Monica, CA.

      Probable Cause, Goldie Paley Gallery, Moore College of Art, Philadelphia, PA.

1990   *MOVE?,* Los Angeles Center for Photographic Studios, Los Angeles, CA.

1989   *Brokenhearted,* Jamaica Arts Center, New York, NY.

      Political Varieties, Fayerweather Gallery, University of Virginia, Charlottesville, VA.

**Meditations on Discovering That I Hear
My Mother When I Talk to My Daughter**   1993

Selected Group Exhibitions
1994   *The Fifth Havana Biennial: Art, Society, and Reflection,* The National Museum of Fine Arts and The Wilfredo Lam Centre, Havana, Cuba.

1993   *Personal Narratives: Women Photographers of Color,* Southeastern Center for Contemporary Art, Winston-Salem, NC.

      The Biennial at the Whitney Museum of American Art, New York, NY.

The Visual Diary, Houston Center for Photography, Houston, TX.

1992   *Bridges and Boundaries: African Americans and American Jews,* The Jewish Museum, New York, NY.

Re-Framings, Randolph Street Gallery, Chicago, IL.

Dirt and Domesticity: Constructions of the Feminine, Whitney Museum of American Art, New York, NY.

Beyond Glory: Re-Presenting Terrorism, Maryland Institute College of Art, Baltimore, MD.

No Justice, No Peace? California Afro-American Museum, Los Angeles, CA.

1991   *Nnommo: Spirit of the Word,* Bomani Gallery, San Francisco, CA.

Diversity and Ethnicity, The Center for Photography at Woodstock, Woodstock, NY.

1990   *The Decade Show,* The New Museum of Contemporary Art, New York, NY.

Family Stories, Snug Harbor Cultural Center, New York, NY.

The Tell-Tale Heart, Washington Project for the Arts, Washington, DC.

The Next Generation, Southeastern Center for Contemporary Art, Winston-Salem, NC.

1989   *Sibling Rivalry,* Tisch School of Art, New York University, New York, NY.

Black Photographers Bear Witness: 100 Years of Social Protest Photography, Williams College Museum of Art, Williamstown, MA.

1988   *Autobiography: In Her Own Image,* INTAR Gallery, New York, NY.

Politically Charged, First Street Forum, St. Louis, MO.

1987   *Race and Representation,* Hunter College, New York, NY.

Image/Identity, Maryland Art Place, Baltimore, MD.

Selected Awards/Grants

1990   NEA Photography Fellowship.

1988   City Arts Individual Artists Grant, Mayor's Advisory Committee on Art and Culture, Baltimore, MD.

NEA/Mid-Atlantic Regional Visual Arts Fellowship for Works on Paper.

1985-
1987   Ford Foundation Grant.

Selected Bibliography

Braziller, George. *Bridges and Boundaries: African Americans and American Jews.* Catalogue. New York: The Jewish Museum, 1992.

Heyman, Abigail. *Flesh and Blood: Photographers' Images Of Their Own Families.* New York: The Picture Project, 1992.

Lippard, Lucy. *Mixed Blessings.* New York: Pantheon Books, 1990.

Pat Ward Williams: Probable Cause. Catalogue. Philadelphia, PA: Moore College of Art, 1992.

Personal Narratives: Women Photographers of Color. Catalogue. Winston-Salem, NC: Southeastern Center for Contemporary Art, 1993.

Florence Flo Oy Wong

As a contemporary mixed media artist, I speak visually, using self-reflective symbols. I contemporize these symbols which are rooted in my bi-cultural life as an American artist of Chinese descent. To reinforce this bi-culturalism, I employ English and Chinese text in pattern and design. Because I want my audience to have access to my use of Chinese, I take the responsibility of explaining my use of Chinese words in my art products. I also display fresh and dried foods, adding a natural element to my aesthetic voice. This voice is a narrative one which focuses on ordinary people and their extraordinary stories. I use colors in both Western and Chinese ways. Red, for me, is cultural and when I use it, I usually indicate good luck. My final works of art are varied as I draw, sew, and paint to bring out that which is deeply ensconced within me as a human being interested in touching myself and others.

What happens when a person nurtures passion for life in heart and mind?
Who or what are the aesthetic agents that provide the emotional recollections in our lives?
How do we reimage the impact of another's actions?
Does that retelling affect others?
Why should we care?

The visual installation of *The Baby Jack Rice Story* explores my responses to the above questions on a personal level. Throughout the years of my marriage to Edward K. Wong, my husband, Ed has inspired me with his recounting of a childhood sustained. I was a willing listener as he "spun his yarn." I noticed that others were deeply engaged as well when Ed shared his reminiscing.

Continuing the use of rice, rice sacks, and hand-sewing, I visually narrate the *Baby Jack Rice* story. I employ photo-realism to depict elements of the telling. Photo-realism also functions as the main video tool, allowing nostalgia to thread the persistence of research. In our use of the colloquial Cantonese phrase, *bay min**, we give written form to *po toong wah***, the language that Ed and I grew up with as Americans.

Artistically, I *bay min** to Robert Rauschenberg and Faith Ringgold. Years ago, when I viewed Rauschenberg's serigraphy on cardboard boxes, I knew he spoke to me. Faith Ringgold's *Quilt Series* which employ textile, text, and sewing gave me courage. Their energies spurred me on to art of my own.

Born
1938   Oakland, CA.

Resides In
Sunnyvale, CA.

Education
1980-   Foothill College, Los Altos Hills, CA.
1982

*Bay Min is colloquial third dialect Cantonese (som yup) which means to give face. Roughly translated, it means to show respect.

**Po Toong Wah is Cantonese for common language which is spoken but not written.

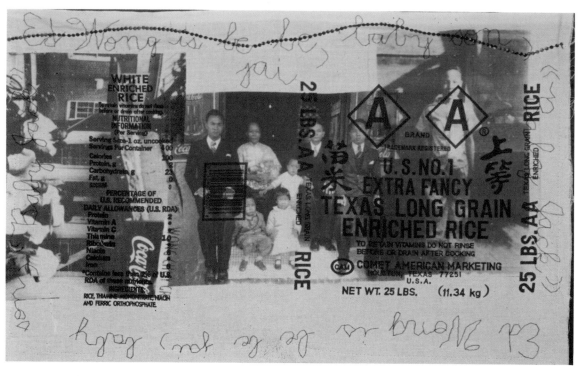

Ed Wong is Be Be Jai 1993

1978- DeAnza College, Cupertino, CA.
1980

1960- California teaching credentials, California State
1961   University Hayward, CA.

1956- B.A., English, University of California, Berkeley, CA.
1960

Selected Solo Exhibitions

1994 *Baby Jack Rice Installation,* San Jose City College, San Jose, CA.

1993 *Rice Story, Eye of the Rice: Yu Mai Gee Fon.* Installation. IDEA Gallery, Sacramento, CA.

1992 *Kaleidoscope,* Prieto Gallery, Mills College, Oakland, CA.

1991 *Long Grain, Extra Fancy,* 1078 Gallery, Chico, CA.

1989 *Chinatown, Et Al.,* Mid-Peninsula YWCA, Palo Alto, CA.

Selected Group Exhibitions

1994 *Domestic Landscapes,* Falkirk Gallery, San Rafael, CA.

Mirror, Mirror: Gender Roles and the Historical Significance of Beauty, California Arts and Craft College, Oakland, CA.

Narratives, Painted Bride Art Center, Philadelphia, PA.

Struggles Against Racism, Cambridge Multicultural Art Center, Cambridge, MA.

1993 *Redefining Self: Six Asian American Artists,* San Jose State University, San Jose, CA.

Diversity-Influences, Creative Growth Center Gallery, Oakland, CA.

1992 *Food For Thought,* Berkeley Art Center Association, Berkeley, CA.

deFORMATION transFORMATION, Hilda Shum, Florence Wong, Capp Street Project, San Francisco, CA.

1991 *Out of the Classroom into the Gallery,* Museum of Children's Art, Oakland, CA.

Our History, Our Rituals, a SALAD BAR Exhibition. Intercultural Gallery, Sonoma State University, Rohnert Park, CA; Bayview Opera House, San Francisco, CA.

1990 *Art as Social Comment,* Brockman Gallery, Los Angeles, CA.

Selected Awards/Grants

1994 Artist in Residence, Villa Montalvo, Saratoga, CA.

1993 Artist in Residence, Headlands Center for the Arts, Sausalito, CA

1992 The Fourth R: Art and the Needs of Children and Youth Award, Euphrat Gallery, DeAnza College, Cupertino, CA.

1991 Asian American Women Artists Association Co-Founders Award.

Selected Public Collections

East Bay Development Center, Oakland, CA.

San Francisco Art Commission, San Francisco, CA.

Selected Bibliography

Bluitt, Kim. "Artist's Work Reflects Heritage," *The Stanford Daily,* Nov. 3, 1989.

Davis, Randal. "Defining Moments: Florence Flo Oy Wong at IDEA," *Artweek,* June 3, 1993, p. 28.

Lee, Bobbie. "Rice Sacks Make For Interesting Artwork," *Asian Week,* May 1992.

Lim, Gerard. "Get Deformed and Transformed Through Rice, Feet And Bullets," *Asian Week,* June 26, 1992.

Lindstrom, Suzan. "Flo Wong: Exploring the Inner House Through Art," *Valley Journal,* April 24, 1991.

Matthews, Lydia. "Stories History Didn't Tell Us," *Artweek,* February 14, 1991.

McCann, Cecile Nelkin. "A conversation with Florence Flo Oy Wong," *Artweek,* June 3, 1993, pp. 28-29.

Muto, Sheila. "Bitter Lesson To Be Learned In Wong's 'Bitter Melon Rice Blues,'" *Asian Week,* July 31, 1992.

Roth, Moira, and Diane Tani. *Flo Oy Wong.* Catalogue in conjunction with Mills College's Kaleidoscope Exhibition. Berkeley, CA: Visibility Press, 1992.

"There's More to Being Chinese in America than Chop Suey: Narrative Drawing as Criticism in Oakland Chinatown," *Pluralistic Approaches to Art Criticism,* Kristin G. Congdon and Doug Blandy, eds. Bowling Green Press, 1992.

Wong, Florence Flo Oy. "Threading Vulnerability: From Quilt to Quilt to Quilts," *Women Educators III,* Kristin Congdon and Enid Zimmerman, eds. Bloomington, IN: School of Education, Indiana University, 1993.

Checklist

Albert Chong
b. 1958   Kingston, Jamaica

**Addressing the Chinese Jamaican
Business Community**
1991
Gelatin silver print with inscribed
copper mat
52.1 x 68.6 cm (20.5 x 27 in.)

Courtesy of the Artist

The Sisters
1994
Hand colored gelatin silver print with
inscribed copper mat
69.9 x 55.9 cm (27.5 x 22 in.)

Courtesy of the Artist

Throne for the Ancestors
1990
Gelatin silver print
101.6 x 76.2 cm (40 x 30 in.)

Courtesy of the Artist

Throne for the Justice
1990

Gelatin silver print
101.6 x 76.2 cm (40 x 30 in.)

Courtesy of the Artist

**Throne for the Keeper of the
Boneyard**
1991
Gelatin silver print with copper mat
101.6 x 76.2 cm (40 x 30 in.)

Courtesy of the Artist and The Carla
Stellweg Gallery, New York, NY

The Two Sisters*
1994
Hand colored gelatin silver print with
incised copper mat
68.6 x 52.1 cm (27 x 20.5 in.)

Courtesy of the Artist

Fay Pullen Fairbrother
b. 1947   New Orleans, LA

The Shroud Series: Quilt Shroud I*
1992
Luminous photographic linen,

100% cotton fabric
Quilt top designed, made, and
photographic transfers by Fay Pullen
Fairbrother
Four African American family portraits,
four African American lynchings;
one white family, two KKK activities,
male and female.
274.3 x 188 cm (108 x 74 in.)

Courtesy of the Artist

The Shroud Series: Quilt Shroud II
1992
Luminous photographic linen, 100%
cotton fabric (overdyed)
Quilt top designed, made, and photo-
graphic transfers by Fay Pullen Fairbrother
Top handquilted by Fay Pullen Fairbrother
Quilt handquilted top to bottom by
L. McCurry
Lynching of African Americans.
274.3 x 188 cm (108 x 74 in.)

Courtesy of the Artist

*Shown in catalog

Lonnie Graham
b. 1954   Cleveland, OH

In A Spirit House: Aunt Dora's Room*
1993
Space of 3.05 x 3.05 m (10 x 10 ft.)

Lonnie Graham wanted to address the issues of spirituality by assaulting the viewer with sight, sound, and memories. After encountering the spiritual manifestation of his Aunt Dora, Lonnie Graham addresses the family and how it continues to affect us. *Aunt Dora's Room* evokes a tangible environment of remembrance and honor.

Courtesy of the Artist in collaboration with the Fabric Workshop, Philadelphia, PA

David Keating
b. 1962   Rye, NY

Family Legend*
1992
Toned gelatin silver print: 55.9 x 86.4 cm (22 x 34 in.)
Antique frame: 68.6 x 99 cm (27 x 39 in.)
Three photoengraved magnesium text panels: 17.8 x 20.3 cm (7 x 8 in.)

94 x 99 cm (37 x 39 in.) overall

Courtesy of the Artist

Troth
1991
Five cibachrome images: 20.3 x 30.5 cm (8 x 12 in.) each
Five high silver-leafed maple frames: 33 x 43.2 cm (13 x 17 in.) each
Five photoengraved magnesium text panels: 10.2 x 25.4 cm (4 x 10 in.) each
101.6 x 149.9 cm (40 x 59 in.) overall

Courtesy of the Artist

Fern Logan
b. 1945   Queens, NY

American Hero*
1992
Cyanotype, van dyke, and oil pastel
111.8 x 88.9 cm (44 x 35 in.)

Courtesy of the Artist

Questions
1992
Cyanotype and van dyke prints on wrapping paper and water color paper
99.1 x 88.9 cm (39 x 35 in.)

Courtesy of the Artist

Lynn Marshall-Linnemeier
b. 1954   Southern Pines, NC

Sanctuary Series
1991
Acrylic on gelatin silver print
Text
Eight pieces
27.9 x 35.6 cm (11 x 14 in.) each print
81.3 x 66 cm (32 x 26 in.) overall

Courtesy of the Artist and
Lucinda W. Bunnen, Atlanta, GA

Sometimes I Hear Voices*
1992
Illuminated photograph (acrylic paint on gelatin silver print)
24.1 x 37.5 cm (19 1/2 x 14 3/4 in.)

Courtesy of the Artist and Drs. Albert and Gail Holloway, Montgomery, AL

Lorie Novak
b. 1954   Los Angeles, CA

Collected Visions*
1993
A three part slide and music installation that examines the representations of women and girls in family photographs and the experience of growing up female.

Slide and Music Installation by Lorie Novak with music by Elizabeth Brown

Collected Visions was commissioned by the Houston Center for Photography with funds from The National Endowment for the Arts.

Lorna Simpson
b. 1960   Brooklyn, NY

Coiffure*
1991
Three gelatin silver develop-out prints, 109.2 x 83.8 cm (43 x 33 in.) each
10 plastic plaques
182.9 x 269.2 cm (72 x 106 in.) overall
1 of 3 editions

In the Collection of the Corcoran Gallery of Art, Gift of the Women's Committee of the Corcoran Gallery of Art, Washington, DC

Clarissa Sligh
b. Washington, D.C.

What's Happening With Momma?
1988
Artist Book

Silkscreen acrylic ink on 100% rag soft white coventry paper
Handset in 10 point Century Schoolbook on 100% rag cream Stonehenge paper
27.9 x 91.4 cm (11 x 36 in.)

Courtesy of the Artist

You Play in Your Good Clothes
from *Reading Dick and Jane with Me*
1989
Crayon on cyanotype on 100% rag Stonehenge natural paper
101.6 x 76.2 cm (40 x 30 in.)

Courtesy of the Artist

Witness Figure With Children
from *Reading Dick and Jane with Me*
1989
Crayon on cyanotype on 100% rag stonehenge natural paper
101.6 x 76.2 cm (40 x 30 in.)

Courtesy of the Artist

Play With Jane
from *Reading Dick and Jane with Me*
1988
Silkscreen on paper
27.9 x 33 cm (11 x 13 in.)
40.6 x 50.8 cm (16 x 20 in.) overall

Courtesy of the Artist

Sandy Ground*
1992–1994
House frame, approximately 2.4 m (8 ft.)
Plaster white sculpture
Cyanotype prints on 100% rag Stonehenge natural paper
Map of Staten Island
Thorns

This piece honors the historic Staten Island fishing village, Sandy Ground—one of the oldest surviving settlements of freed blacks in the nation. The center of *Sandy Ground* is Eliza Morriss Cooler (1800-1884), a free black woman who bought her husband out of slavery, moved north to Sandy Ground in 1830 and raised five children alone after her husband's death at the age of 32 two years later. A large house frame stands over the a large painted map of Staten Island. A sculpture of a woman stands where the town would be on the map.

Courtesy of the Artist and Snug Harbor Cultural Center, Newhouse Center for Contemporary Art, Staten Island, NY

Margaret Stratton
b. 1953   Seattle, WA

Inventory of My Mother's House*
1990-1991
75 gelatin silver prints
Fiber on foamcore
35.6 x 27.9 cm (14 x 11 in.) each print

Courtesy of the Artist

Diane Tani
b. 1965   San Francisco, CA

Bad Words
1988
Plexiglass photo sculpture
Chromogenic print, text
8.9 x 13 x 5.4 cm (3 1/2 x 5 1/8 x 2 1/8 in.)
Installation: 40.6 x 52 x 27.9 cm
(16 x 20 1/2 x 11 in.)

Courtesy of the Artist

Forever Foreign
1989
Chromogenic print
Text by Kimiko Hahn
50.8 x 40.6 cm (20 x 16 in.)

Courtesy of the Artist

Stereotype
1989
Chromogenic print, text
40.6 x 50.8 cm (16 x 20 in.)

Courtesy of the Artist

Self-Identity*
1989
Chromogenic print, text
40.6 x 50.8 cm (16 x 20 in.)

Courtesy of the Artist

Christian Walker
b. 1954   Springfield, MA

**Bargaining with the Dead:
Great Grandmother, Uncles, Aunt***
1986–88
Pigment on gelatin silver print, varnish
40.6 x 50.8 cm (16 x 20 in.)

Courtesy of Lucinda W. Bunnen,
Atlanta, GA

**Bargaining with the Dead:
Grandmother, Grandfather, Aunts**
1986–88
Pigment on gelatin silver print, varnish
40.6 x 50.8 cm (16 x 20 in.)

Courtesy of Lucinda W. Bunnen,
Atlanta, GA

**Bargaining with the Dead:
Mother, Grandmother, Uncle**
1986–88
Pigment on gelatin silver print, varnish
40.6 x 50.8 cm (16 x 20 in.)

Courtesy of Lucinda W. Bunnen,
Atlanta, GA

**Bargaining with the Dead:
Mother, Grandmother, Father**
1986–88
Pigment on gelatin silver print, varnish
40.6 x 50.8 cm (16 x 20 in.)

Courtesy of Lucinda W. Bunnen,
Atlanta, GA

**Bargaining with the Dead:
Mother**
1986–88
Pigment on gelatin silver print, varnish
40.6 x 50.8 cm (16 x 20 in.)

Courtesy of Lucinda W. Bunnen,
Atlanta, GA

**Bargaining with the Dead:
Mother, Brothers, Nephew**
1986–88

Pigment on gelatin silver print, varnish
40.6 x 50.8 cm (16 x 20 in.)

Courtesy of Lucinda W. Bunnen,
Atlanta, GA

Carrie Mae Weems
b. 1953   Portland, OR

1990
Untitled (Woman and daughter with makeup)
Gelatin silver print: 69.2 x 69.2 cm
(27 1/4 x 27 1/4 in.)
text panels: 27.9 x 27.9 cm (11 x 11 in.)

Courtesy of the Artist and P.P.O.W. Gallery,
New York, NY

1990
Untitled (Woman with daughter)
Left triptych panel
Gelatin silver print: 69.2 x 69.2 cm
(27 1/4 x 27 1/4 in.)
text panels: 27.9 x 27.9 cm (11 x 11 in.)

Courtesy of the Artist and P.P.O.W. Gallery,
New York, NY

1990
Untitled (Woman with daughter)*
Center triptych panel
Gelatin silver print: 69.2 x 69.2 cm
(27 1/4 x 27 1/4 in.
text panels: 27.9 x 27.9 cm (11 x 11 in.)

Courtesy of the Artist and P.P.O.W. Gallery,
New York, NY

1990
Untitled (Woman with daughter)
Right triptych panel
Gelatin silver print: 69.2 x 69.2 cm
(27 1/4 x 27 1/4 in.)
text panels: 27.9 x 27.9 cm (11 x 11 in.)

Courtesy of the Artist and P.P.O.W. Gallery,
New York, NY

1990
Untitled (Woman and daughter with
children)
Gelatin silver print: 69.2 x 69.2 cm
(27 1/4 x 27 1/4 in.)
text panels: 27.9 x 27.9 cm (11 x 11 in.)

Courtesy of the Artist and P.P.O.W. Gallery,
New York, NY

Pat Ward Williams
b. 1948   Philadelphia, PA

**Meditations on Discovering That
I Hear My Mother When I Talk to
My Daughter***
1993
Dot-screen mural photograph
Color photography
Mixed media
381 x 487.7 cm (150 x 192 in.)

Courtesy of the Artist

Florence Flo Oy Wong
b. 1938   Oakland, CA

Baby Jack Rice Story
1993
Serigraphy, sequins, thread on cloth
rice and flour sacks
253.4 x 172.7 cm (93¾ x 68 in.) overall
"To Bay Min: The Baby Jack Rice Story,"
a 10 minute video production

**Soon after Wong Yet Choy and
Sue Shee**
50.8 x 81.3 cm (20 x 32 in.)

**Baby Jack Rice
Red and Gold Sequins**
50.8 x 81.3 cm (20 x 32 in.)

The Corner Beckoned
73.7 x 86.4 cm (29 x 34 in.)

Don't tell Momma
50.8 x 81.3 cm (20 x 32 in.)

In 1930 SueShee Wong Came
50.8 x 81.3 cm (20 x 32 in.)

Ed Wong is Be Be Jai* (detail)
50.8 x 81.3 cm (20 x 32 in.)

They weren't supposed to be friends
50.8 x 81.3 cm (20 x 32 in.)

You gotta be brave
75.9 x 86.4 cm (29 7/8 x 34 in.)

Courtesy of the Artist

Acknowledgments

The planning of the National African American Museum has been facilitated and supported during the past four years by the Secretary of the Smithsonian, Robert McCormick Adams, Constance Newman, Under Secretary, Tom Freudenheim, Assistant Secretary for Arts and Humanities, his former Deputy, Elaine Heumann Gurian, and current office staff: Priscilla Brown, Beth Fisher, Rick Haas, Rafael A. Pena; Alice Green Burnett, Assistant Secretary for Institutional Initiatives; James Early, Assistant Secretary for Education and Public Service; Robert Hoffman, Assistant Secretary for Science and his Deputy Ross Simons; Tom Lovejoy, Assistant Secretary for External Affairs and his Deputy Marc Pachter, Nancy Suttenfield, Assistant Secretary for Finance and Administration; Richard Siegle, Director of Facilities Service and Carol Wharton, Director of the Office of Planning and Budget.

The National African American Museum's first exhibition was made possible because of generous contributions for the exhibition, catalog and public programs from The Smithsonian Institution Special Exhibition Fund, the Educational Outreach Fund and the Office of Fellowships and Grants. Our deepest gratitude is expressed to the Geraldine R. Dodge Foundation and Price Waterhouse.

The exhibition received cooperation from a number of individuals and galleries. We would like to thank the participating artists along with those who generously loan works for *Imagining Families*: the Corcoran Gallery of Art, the P.P.O.W. Gallery, Houston Center for Contemporary Photography, Jackson Fine Art Gallery, Southeast Center for Contemporary Art, MacIntosh Gallery, Carla Stellweg Gallery, Southeast Museum of Photography, Phillip Brookman, Kellie Jones, Lucinda W. Bunnen, Drs. Albert and Gail Holloway, Newhouse Center for Contemporary Art, Snug Harbor Cultural Center.

We are especially indebted to the designers who have worked on the exhibition and accompanying publications. We would like to thank our exhibition designer, Veronica Jackson along with Peter Gallagher and Terry Healy of Douglas/Gallagher; John Morning of John Morning Design, Inc. and The Eisenman Press for the exhibition catalog; and Jonathan Pressler for installing the exhibition.

We would like to extend our gratitude to the staff, interns, and fellows of the National African American Museum for their tireless work in presenting this exhibition: Frieda Austin, Deirdre Cross, Shireen Dodson, Dottie Green, Jane Lusaka, Kemp Powers, Shirley Solomon, Ann Walker, and Mark Wright; Bridget Cooks, Shiho Fukui, Sam Roberts, and Shawn Saunders; and Jonathan Holloway, Ben Kinard, Robert Poarch.

The National African American Museum has a very small staff. This exhibition would not have been possible without the collective effort of teams of individuals throughout the Smithsonian who supported our work. We would like to thank Tracey Cones and the Building Management staff; John Coppola, Tim Smith, and the staff of the Office of Exhibits Central; Michael Sofield and the staff of the Office of Plant Services; Aris T. Allen, Judd McIntire and the staff of the Office of Design and Construction; Jan Majewski, Accessibility Coordinator, Office for the Assistant Secretary for the Arts and Humanities; Herman Thompson and the staff of the Office of Printing and Photographic Services; Patrick Scars, John Zelenik, Tom Moriarty and the design staff of the Sackler and Freer Galleries; Ed Ryan, Margaret Grandine, and the registration staff of the 1876 Centennial Exhibition, National Museum of American History; and the Office of Public Affairs. We are also grateful for the on-going support of John Brown and the Office of Development and Rachelle Browne and the office of the General Counsel.

This exhibition is dedicated to the memory of Carmen Turner, Under Secretary of the Smithsonian Institution and

Robert Burke, Director of the Office of Protection Service. Mrs. Turner and Mr. Burke were members of the initial Advisory Board that conceptualized a framework for the National African American Museum. They supported us through their words as well as their acts. We give honor to their lives and their work; for as we imagine families, we know of no better role-models to guide our efforts in the years ahead.

— Claudine K. Brown
Deputy Assistant Secretary
for the Arts and Humanities,
Smithsonian Institution

— Deborah Willis
Curator